"Dr. McClone has somehow been able to take the best that various spiritual practices and philosophies have to offer and weave them together with the uniting thread of psychology. The result is an informed and integrated approach to personal transformation. To be sure this is not another prosaic self-help book—not even close. *The Road to Joy* is qualitatively different. It is built on examples from diverse origins, informed from clinical experience, and contextualized in a concise tome that is as actionable as it is inspiring. I highly recommend it."

—**CHRIS E. STOUT**
Associate Professor of International Psychology,
Chicago School of Professional Psychology

"Dr. McClone, not to be confused with McGlone, has given us an extraordinary and timely book. This should be required reading in these pandemic times. He beautifully integrates the research with storytelling and practical ways to be, know, and become JOY! It is and will be something one can read and re-read in prayer, meditation, or silence each day and discover another jewel."

—**GERARD J. MCGLONE, SJ**
Senior Research Fellow, Berkley Center for Religion,
Peace and World Affairs, Georgetown University

"Combining tender stories of the author's own experiences with wisdom from both spiritual sages and contemporary scientists, McClone offers an abundance of clues to guide us on our lifelong journey to authentic happiness. He shows how even the unwanted realities of pain, failure, and grief may open the door to deeper life. In this book, we will recognize the voice of one who has 'walked the walk' of search, suffering, compassion, and care."

—**MARY FROHLICH, RSCJ**
Professor of Spirituality, Catholic Theological Union

"In *The Road to Joy* Kevin McClone, a seasoned psychologist, highlights in a warm, engaging style eight pathways to a fuller, more joyful life. Those confronting addictions in themselves or their families of origin will be especially interested in McClone's example-filled discussions of honesty and integrity. We appreciated the 'Action Plans' at the end of each chapter and especially enjoyed chapters on vulnerability and one with the title of 'Simplify, Simplify.'"

—JAMES AND EVELYN WHITEHEAD
Authors of *Holy Eros: Pathways to a Passionate God*

"This lovely book is the result of the wisdom and gentleness that are fruits of a life lived honestly and lovingly, and fruits as well of the deep suffering that only loving and honesty can bring. Readers will feel themselves blessed that Kevin McClone has been able to share so much of his own life's journey in a way that both inspires and challenges them, and leads them to the joy that he himself has found."

—STEPHEN B. BEVANS, SVD
Louis J. Luzbetak, SVD, Professor of Mission and Culture,
Catholic Theological Union

"Spiritual growth is difficult. Kevin McClone has written a helpful guide, sharing portions of his own journey along with rich insights from psychology and ancient and modern spiritual masters from diverse traditions."

—GEORGE FITCHETT
Director, Transforming Chaplaincy

"Gathering up and weaving together the insights of wisdom figures from the worlds of psychology and spirituality, Kevin McClone has produced a guide for joyful living. The reflections in each chapter function as pathways that lead to that joy. Drawn from McClone's decades of pastoral ministry, his training in psychology, and his own ongoing search for authenticity, these reflections probe the very depths of the human desire for meaning. By speaking from his own experience, McClone demonstrates the openness and honesty needed as one travels this road to joy."

—DIANNE BERGANT
CSA, Carroll Stuhlmueller, CP, Distinguished Professor Emerita
of Old Testament Studies, Catholic Theological Union

The Road to Joy

The Road to Joy

Eight Pathways of Psychospiritual Transformation

By KEVIN P. McCLONE

WIPF & STOCK · Eugene, Oregon

THE ROAD TO JOY
Eight Pathways of Psychospiritual Transformation

Wipf & Stock
An Imprint of Wipf and Stock Publishers
199 W. 8th Ave., Suite 3
Eugene, OR 97401

www.wipfandstock.com

PAPERBACK ISBN: 978-1-7252-6358-1
HARDCOVER ISBN: 978-1-7252-6359-8
EBOOK ISBN: 978-1-7252-6360-4

Manufactured in the U.S.A.   JUNE 4, 2020

Contents

Introduction

As THIS BOOK, THE *Road to Joy*, is in its final preparation for publication, we find ourselves face to face with the coronavirus global pandemic. This universal experience seems to have shattered many of our worldviews. Faced with so many things we were powerless over, many were tempted to despair. Rates of anxiety and depression were on the rise and a search for meaning and ways to cope became paramount. Many persons were forced to reassess their priorities and attend to those things that matter most.

Out of this liminal experience we came to experience our common mortality and that which matters most often appeared in clearer view. This often led to acts of care and love toward family, friends and reaching out to those who were most vulnerable in self-less acts of service and love. This was especially true of so many health-care workers who risked so much for all of us. The new realities facing so many in this global pandemic reminded us of some universal realities that we often avoid seeing, that we are less in control then we think, that what is most essential in life is often invisible to the eye and that the measure of a person often is revealed through adversity.

In my over twenty years as a clinical psychologist, certified chaplain, teacher, and alcohol and drug counselor, my work and ministry has immersed me into questions surrounding those principles that lead to more lasting peace, serenity and true joy of living. This book will highlight eight core pathways that lead to such a psychospiritual transformation into joy. A core Cambridge dictionary definition describes transformation as a complete change in the character of something or someone, especially so that thing or person is improved. It is this sense of transformation toward meaningful psychospiritual growth that this book refers.

For much of my life, my wife Grace and I have sought to weave insights from the fields of psychology and spirituality into our life, clinical work, pastoral ministry and teaching. When my wife of twenty-eight years passed away two years ago, I found myself alone with my thoughts of the legacy of life and love she left me. In our lives, such experiences of deep loss and grief shatter our world as we know it and often leads us to contemplate the deeper essence of what makes life meaningful and worthwhile. My wife, Grace, was one of those rare people who radiate true joy. This was not only my experience, but the experience of the hundreds of people she came into contact with in her teaching, counseling, and ministry activities.

The Road to Joy with its eight core pathways may be a useful resource going forward. The Road to Joy doesn't seek to escape suffering but rather to discover deeper meaning in amidst trauma and loss. To discover the virtue of living out of one's deepest desires and truest self is all the more important when we are forced through suffering to reevaluate how we are all connected to each other. Being faced with limits we reconnect to what matters most. Some of the core pathways that may light that path are accepting our losses and limits by embracing the gifts of faith hope and love. That road is nurtured through simplicity, letting go of non-essentials and embracing our deepest self. Solitude connects us to that deeper center. Joy is living life to the full one day at a time and all that matters is to share that life and love with one another on love and service.

Although I have been a hospice chaplain and have taught graduate-level courses for years on death and dying and loss and grief, this knowledge pales in comparison to experiencing a deep personal loss of a beloved. This book is written in honor of my wife Grace, who deeply embodied many of the eight core pathways of psychospiritual transformation outlined here. I was encouraged by many of my clients, graduate theology students, colleagues and mentors to write this book. My biggest cheerleader is my son, Matthew, who not only encouraged me to write this book, but kept me accountable to the discipline of regular writing.

Why the focus on psychospirituality? Psychospirituality, according to the dictionary, is the relationship between spirituality and the mind or psychology. For my purposes here, psychospirituality of growth refers to psychological and spiritual principles that contribute to more authentic and mature loving that leads to joy. As the years have gone by, I have come to believe ever more deeply that the best psychological and spiritual growth principles come together in the person who is fully alive and able to offer generative love to others. In Western societies, psychological and spiritual development have too long been treated as separate domains. Within the past thirty years, there has been a new interest in the integration of spirituality or faith perspectives and psychology. Science and religion have grown closer together over this same period and there is less distrust in many circles. There is a growing understanding of the critical importance of weaving psychological and spiritual principles together as a guide to healthy maturation. Two areas that have assisted in this have been the positive psychology and transpersonal psychology movements, coupled with more research into mystical and spiritual literature dealing with the importance of oneness, the transcendent, and soulful living, to name a few.

While my writing is informed by my Christian faith, I will be drawing as well from the major spiritual and mystical traditions, including Christian, Jewish, Buddhist and Islamic sources to highlight the universal dimensions of these eight pathways to discovering true joy. I long to better understand how we grow and change as human beings and follow our better angels, not our worst instincts. I invite you to join me on this journey as I share insights gleaned from personal lived experience, psychological research, teaching, and clinical work that speak to these pathways leading to more passionate joyful living. My hope is that these pathways help light our way to grow in faith, hope, and love.

Introduction

The audience for this book is wide and varied. First, this book is for anyone desiring to discover their deepest calling and to embrace life more fully. I endeavor to speak words of comfort, encouragement, and hope to people who struggle with physical, mental, and emotional challenges. I write for those many men and women in recovery from various addictions that have found new life in twelve-step programs as well as those still captive to active addiction. Young people who are searching for deeper answers to life's meaning and purpose may find some resonance here. So many youth today are disillusioned and alienated from political and religious structures that they perceive have failed them. So, for the many young people today deeply committed to a world where they seek to build peace over violence, unity amidst diversity, and bridges over walls, this book is for you.

I am writing as well for the many clients and students that have honored me in openly sharing their struggles, hopes, and fears through these many years. This writing is for the students and mentors at Catholic Theological Union, specifically to the Institute of Religious Formation, the Hesburgh sabbatical program, and our own Institute of Sexuality Studies students who I have been privileged to get to know over these past sixteen years. I have learned so much from their own redemptive stories of growth and transformation. Finally, if you are a seeker of growth, desiring more authentic living, this book is for you. It may be of special interest to those many persons entrusted in their work and pastoral ministry to guide and mentor others along the path of psychospiritual growth, such as teachers, pastoral counselors, religious formators, and pastoral ministers.

Follow Your Deepest Desire

Discover Your Calling

Who looks outside, dreams. Who looks inside, awakens.

—CARL GUSTAV JUNG

WHAT IS THE DEEPEST desire of your heart? Do you sometimes find yourself longing for something more, something of greater depth and meaning? Wilke Au and Noreen Cannon, in their book *Urgings of the Heart*, describe this yearning within our hearts for more, as an openness to transcendence.[1] Yet, despite this longing, I notice in my own life that I both yearn and fear exploring this inward journey. While I desire to live more fully, another part of me fears the demands this stillness or calling may place before me. You may have felt a similar tension in your own conflicting or competing desires.

Psychospiritual growth and transformation begins less by looking outside than by looking inward to deeper levels of meaning, purpose, and life direction. Real change is an inside job and this has been a lasting truth. We live in a world in which people

---

1. Au and Cannon, *Urgings of the Heart,* 10.

struggle for answers as to the purpose and meaning of their existence, as American monk and mystic Thomas Merton aptly notes:

> Our life, as individual persons and as members of a perplexed and struggling race, provokes us with the evidence that it must have meaning. Part of meaning still escapes us. Yet our purpose in life is to discover this meaning and live according to it.[2]

Merton's words echo our human condition and thus have a timeless quality that speaks to our age. Some writers say that discovering deeper meaning and seeking to live by it is finding our vocation. James Martin, SJ, the Jesuit author,[3] states that vocations are developed through desire and especially following our deeper desires. The origin of this sense of vocation comes from the Latin *vocare*, which means "to call." A vocation is something you are called to as much as one seeks. How we discover this vocation can be a long and challenging process. It demands reflection, discernment, and a journeying inward. Looking back on my life, I have spent many restless years avoiding such inner truths. The search for meaning and purpose is fundamentally a journey of mature development and a gift of the spirit.

Seeds of future growth often begin in the heart's longing for something more fulfilling and lasting. The harsh reality is that often we have to experience dissatisfaction, lack of fulfillment, and at times real pain and suffering to truly desire something more and be open to change. Common yearnings I hear voiced in my clinical practice include the yearning to be heard and seen as you are (not for what others want you to be) and the yearning to be accepted (including your imperfections). For others, they may long to escape the pain of loneliness, to discover meaningful work, or to find peace from various stressful life events.

Many clients come to therapy seeking meaning, amidst the loss of meaning. Like I did regarding the loss of my wife, they too struggle to cope, to find meaning after a deep loss in their life.

2. Merton, *No Man Is an Island*, xi.
3. Martin, *Jesuit Guide*, 341.

For others, it may be a feeling of being trapped in the throes of anxiety, depression, or some compulsive pattern that keeps them feeling lost or alone. Such persons come seeking answers that will help them on the path to deeper meaning, to find hope in what seems senseless. The agony of such questioning after a trauma can lead to despair, but at other times, it may lead to transformation. I am so often awed by the graced responses of some parents who have lost sons and daughters to senseless gun violence who speak of love, mercy, forgiveness, and hope, despite their incalculable grief and trauma.

My own experience has been that the answers to life's deepest longings don't come until we name and claim what those deeper desires are. The first pathway of psychospiritual transformation, then, is tapping into these deeper desires and embracing the person we wish to become. So, awakening to our deepest desires allows us to discover meaning by entering the deep. We live in a world of many competing desires and attractions that seem to demand our attention. The different voices of family, career, and self-fulfillment demand our focus and we are not always clear how to channel our time and energy. These questions are not new but rather recur over time immemorial.

When we discover our larger purpose, what gives meaning to our lives, then the challenge is to face this calling with courage and develop the capacity to follow its path. Protestant theologian and existential philosopher Paul Tillich, in his classic work *The Courage to Be*, speaks to this experience when he states, "The vitality that can stand the abyss of meaninglessness is to be aware of a hidden meaning within the destruction of meaning."[4]

Following the deeper desires of our hearts demands a focused single-mindedness that seeks to discern between competing desires. Even a path that at first seems unattractive, upon reflection, may indeed become a better, more authentic path. Seeking answers to the person I most desire to become draws me beyond my own selfish desires to a larger, more transcendent reality. Mystics and spiritual writers from the major religious traditions have

4. Tillich, *Courage to Be*, 177.

long since spoken of the desire to transcend the self and enter into a deeper connection with all of creation. These traditions testify to a larger Unitive reality. The notion of a Oneness of Being takes many forms. This unity is beyond duality but speaks of a connection and oneness with all humanity. For example, in the Christian tradition, "There is neither Jew nor Gentile, neither slave nor free, nor is there male and female, for you are all one in Christ Jesus." (Gal 3:28) From the Hindu classic, the *Bhagavad Gita*, "He who experiences the unity of life sees his own Self in all beings, and all beings in his own Self and looks on everything with an impartial eye; he who sees Me in everything and everything in Me, him shall I never forsake, nor shall he lose Me" and from Islam, "Those who act kindly in this world will have kindness." (Qu'ran 39:10)

This God, who invites us into unitive love, speaks to us in our holy and whole desires. James Martin, SJ, distinguishes "holy desires" from more superficial desires as he states:

> Holy desires are different from surface wants like "I want a new car or I want a new computer." Instead, I'm talking about our deepest desires, the ones that shape our lives; desires that help us know who we are to become and what we are to do.[5]

The challenge here is becoming more real, authentic, and honest with our deeper hopes, dreams, and fears. Even agnostics and atheists have holy desires that reveal themselves in various ways. It may be our longing for completeness or a feeling that we are lacking something. This dissatisfaction doesn't simply have to be endured, but can ultimately lead to a more fulfilled life if faced rather than avoided. Many of us may seek comfort with money, status, or power as a way to fill this emptiness inside, only to end up feeling more lost and alone.

At times we may experience emptiness following experiences of suffering, loss, and grief. After my wife died from lymphoma two years ago, the world as I knew it felt shattered, and I struggled for meaning and direction going forward. I found myself

5. Martin, *Jesuit Guide*, 59.

remembering, savoring, and giving thanks for the precious gift Grace was to me, as a friend, wife, and mother. I felt my faith being shaken, purified, and deepened at different moments of grief and remembrance. At times, my wife felt so close and other times, so far away. I remember telling close friends, "It feels weird, but at times I am more acutely aware of her real essence in her absence." I found solace and hope in these words from C. S. Lewis, who related his own experience of grief at the death of his wife:

> God has not been trying an experiment on my faith or love in order to find out their quality. He knew it already. It was I who didn't. In this trial He makes us occupy the dock, the witness box, and the bench all at once. He always knew that my temple was a house of cards. His only way of making me realize the fact was to knock it down.[6]

Who Grace was for me and how she lived her life is clearer to me now in her physical absence. The essence of her faith, love, and integrity is a living witness that lingers in my heart. Often, such an experience of loss can break us open to see deeper into the essence of our loved ones. These holy witnesses of life, love, and compassion in our lives are the spark that ignites an inward journey which calls us forth to our deepest self.

Psychospiritual transformation that culminates in joyful living involves a process of being present to what is most real in life. I am reminded of the saying by Thomas Merton, from his semi-autobiographical novel *My Argument with the Gestapo*, which has become a sort of guiding light:

> If you want to identify me, ask me not where I live or what I like to eat, or how I comb my hair, but ask me what I think I am living for, in detail, and ask me what I think is keeping me from living fully for the thing I want to live for. Between these two answers you can determine the identity of any person. The better answer he(she) has, the more of a person he(she) is . . . I am all the time trying to make out the answer as I go on living.[7]

6. Lewis, *Grief Observed*, 42–43.

7. Merton, *My Argument with the Gestapo*, 160–61.

My wife's life was a witness to faith, love, and service to others. What do we want our legacy to be?

Reflecting on my own life, those moments of deepest clarity, meaning, and transcendence have happened when I am truly present in the here and now to what is most real and when I seek to respond in love. This is the gift of the precious present moment, which I can embrace or miss entirely. Despite knowing this gift of presence, I can easily find myself drawn into less conscious activities or useless distractions. Perhaps you have a similar love/hate relationship with change and becoming more real. This is the paradoxical nature we as human beings often encounter. For example, as much as I desire to be more real and authentic, my life is often filled with contradictions. I know that I have wasted many hours and days on mindless endeavors that ultimately fail to satisfy. There is always another desire to lure me off course and leave me wanting more and more . . . to be satisfied.

This beautiful, classic story of a Greek fisherman reminds me of how the voices calling for more and more can block us from seeing what is most real right before us.

The story goes like this . . .

A fishing boat docked in a tiny Greek village. A tourist complimented the Greek fisherman on the quality of his fish, and asked how long it took him to catch them. "Oh, not very long," answered the fisherman.

"But then, why didn't you stay in the sea longer and catch more?" the tourist asked.

The Greek man explained that his small catch was more than sufficient to meet his needs and those of his family.

"But what do you do with the rest of your time?" the tourist asked.

"I fish a little, I sleep late, I play with my children, and I take a siesta with my wife. In the evenings, I go into the village to see my friends, to dance a little, I play the bouzouki, and sing a few songs. I have a full life," the fisherman explained.

The tourist interrupted: "I have an MBA from Harvard and I can help you. You should start by fishing all day. Then you can sell the other fish you catch. With the revenue, you can buy a bigger boat. With the extra money, the larger boat will bring more money and you can buy a second one, and a third one, and so on until you have an entire fleet of trawlers. Instead of selling your fish to a middleman, you can negotiate directly with the processing plants, and maybe even open your own plant. You can then leave this little village and move to Athens, London, or even New York. From there, you can control your huge enterprise."

"How long would that take?" asked the fisherman.

"Twenty, perhaps twenty-five years," replied the tourist.

"And after that?" asked the fisherman.

"Afterwards? That's when it gets fascinating! When your business operations get really big, you can start selling shares and make millions!" said the tourist.

"Millions? Really? And after that?" asked the fisherman.

"After that, you'll be ready to retire and go to live in a tiny village near the coast. There you can play with your grandchildren, catch a few fish, take a siesta with your wife, and sleep late. In the evenings, you can spend your time singing, dancing, and playing the bouzouki with your friends!"[8]

In my own life, running after more has generally left me feeling more empty, while I missed the full life right in front of me. We may work hard for a future that will never come because it was always right in front of us but remained unlived. What is stopping you from discovering and embracing what is most real today? The fisherman, by never forgetting what was most precious, by living within his needs, learned the value of authentic and purposeful living. The discovery of what is most precious often comes only after countless detours.

Today, we live in a world of competing desires of a seemingly infinite variety. What do we choose? What desires lie at the center of my soul? What desires lead to a peace that lasts? Desire draws us toward something, but how do we sort through these varied desires and learn more meaningful desires that create more authentic living? We can take the risk to reach out for help, either with a

8. Anonymous.

close friend, twelve-step sponsor, professional guide, spiritual director, mentor, or therapist.

I have observed in retrospect that many people who make the personal choice to come to therapy are often already halfway there. Because they are open to risk, to be vulnerable, to seek growth, they bravely enter the uncharted territory of exploring deeper truths. One of the hardest tasks we have as human beings is to ask for help and yet, when we reach out for help and become vulnerable, our burden is often more manageable. No one of us is an island. Emptiness, alienation, and disconnection are antithetical to the very nature of what it means to be truly human and what it means to be spiritual. When I am connected to the world around me and to the people in my life, I feel more fulfilled.

For many persons like myself, pain often becomes the touchstone to progress, growth, and new possibilities. The question that I often ask my clients in an initial session is, "What is it that you desire most?" Responses vary but some common remarks go something like this: "I am tired of the way my life is going." Whether the struggle is with loss, anxiety, depression, stress at work, or relationship issues, each person comes longing for greater peace, meaning, and hope for the future. In seeking help, we find ourselves less guarded in facing lower level desires that leave us empty.

We often desire things that can actually impair happiness rather than foster it. A man in recovery from addiction shared with me how he realized his higher power was alcohol and drugs because it became his primary desire, what he always thought about, and where he spent all his time and energy, until it nearly killed him. Another writer, Caroline Knapp, in her autobiographical book *Drinking: A Love Story*, describes in vivid detail how her love for alcohol was akin to the drink becoming her primary relationship, as she wrote:

> Yes; this is a love story. . . I loved the way drink made me
> feel, and I loved its special power of deflection, its ability
> to shift my focus away from my own awareness of self

and onto something else, something less painful than my own feelings.[9]

This first foundational pathway of psychospiritual growth is about awakening to the deepest desires of our heart and realizing that fullness of living and loving comes not by acquiring more but by doing with less, by letting go of the superficial or false pursuits. It is becoming a servant of the whole, where growth is waking up to what matters and having the courage to pursue that inward journey. A journey more of letting go than endless pursuit. Twenty-five hundred years ago, the famous Chinese philosopher Lao Tzu wrote:

> In the pursuit of learning, every day something is acquired.
> In the pursuit of Tao, every day something is dropped.
> Less and less is done
> Until non-action is achieved.
> When nothing is done, nothing is left undone.
> The world is ruled by letting things take their course.
> It cannot be ruled by interfering.[10]

The Chinese principle of "wu wei" literally means "to do nothing is to do something." It is one of the great paradoxes of life that perhaps makes sense only in the realm of the spiritual life. It is an inward journey of letting go of all our striving and being fully present to what is most real. This concept reminds me of a time that I was arguing with my wife about running late for a wedding. I was anxious not to be late, which to me would be disrespectful. After some pressure, she finally remarked, "Don't worry, Kevin, if our hearts are there we are already there." My anxiety about not being late kept me from focusing on what really mattered.

Most of the major religious and spiritual traditions speak to this awakening to our deepest desires as what ultimately leads to greater awareness, love, and a feeling of Oneness. Consider some of the following quotes:

9. Knapp, *Drinking*, 7.
10. Tzu, *Tao Teh Ching*, ch. 48.

I consider myself a Hindu, Moslem, Jew, Buddhist and Confucian.
—Mahatma Gandhi

Truth is one. Sages call it by different names.
—*Rig Veda*, 4000 BC

We carry inside us the wonders we seek outside us.
—Rumi

Walk as if you are kissing the Earth with your feet.
—Thich Nhat Hanh, Buddhist monk

What these spiritual writers have in common is their reverence for the inner soul journey to uncover our interconnected feeling of oneness with all humanity. We are all part of one another and our diversity is our strength, not weakness.

Holy Grace of Desire

Michael Casey, a Trappist monk, speaks of the holy grace of desire. Quoting Thomas Aquinas, he reminds us that three things are necessary for the salvation of man (woman): "To know what he ought to believe; to know what he ought to desire; and to know what he ought to do." For Casey, "Desire is like a springboard."[11] We know our departure point, but we do not know where we are going to end up. We desire what is beyond. The paradox is that this invisible reality has a dynamic power of attraction that has the effect of energizing us to search more deeply. It is not a fantasy; it is not a delusion. Its reality can be verified by the energy it imparts.

Deeper desires are discovered in awakening to the soul moments of our life. These holy moments, sometimes referred to as "Aha!" moments, are what Christians refer to as *kairos* moments that can open the door to transformation and grace. *Kairos* (used eighty-six times in the New Testament) refers to an opportune time, a "moment" or a "season," whereas *chronos* (used fifty-four times) refers to a specific amount of time, such as a day or an hour. Much of our time is chronological or sequential time, immersed

---

11. Casey, *Grace*, 21.

with activity, responsibilities, and daily routines. Time becomes a commodity. A deeper experience of time is *kairos* time. Those who have reported such self-transcending *kairos* experiences report altered states of consciousness with a heightened awareness, which speaks to an opportune time for action, often an in-breaking of the divine. It may be at these times that we feel called to some deeper reality. While *chronos* is more quantitative, *kairos* is more qualitative and can awaken us to the threshold of change, growth, and new realities.

When exploring how to cultivate deeper desires, we have a wealth of wisdom from psychological and spiritual resources. I recently heard powerful testimony at a presentation at Catholic Theological Union from a panel of nine men who were all released from prison after serving from ten to thirty years for crimes, mostly committed in their teenage years.[12] I recall in particular one man's heartwrenching story that it was only in looking back now, many years later, he could see more clearly what happened. He grew up in a single-parent family. His older brother, who he looked up to, dealt drugs, and early on he was drawn into that life, which to him seemed inevitable. He shared that he had no real positive role models. Like most young children, he desired security, belonging, and so he did what his older brother trained him to do. He did a good job and recalled that initially he felt some affirmation and esteem from his success, albeit misguided. His deep desire now, after years of imprisonment, is to help other young men trapped in the cycle of violence and drugs to not follow that path and end up in prison. Like one young man on the panel of ex-prisoners stated, "Those of us who hurt, hurt others." But what I heard in his testimony was those who feel love and care can become the wounded healers of our world. Love and care for others draws us closer to our deepest calling that we are one among many.

We are often our own worst enemies with competing desires. We spend so much time, money, and energy on what ultimately fails to satisfy. Parker Palmer, in his most recent book *On the Brink*

---

12. David Kelly, "Communities and Relatives of Illinois Incarcerated Children" (panel, Catholic Theological Union, Chicago, IL, January 14, 2019).

of Everything, explores various types of desire and comes to the conclusion that "The desire to 'hang on' comes from a sense of scarcity and fear. The desire to 'give myself' comes from a sense of abundance and generosity."[13] That is why desire, in its purest form, is a grace that allows us to move beyond more selfish desires. Do you view life in terms of scarcity or abundance? Is your cup empty or overflowing?

Joan Chittister, a Benedictine theologian and Scripture scholar, writes that "Life grows us more and more, but only if we wrestle daily with its ever-daily meaning for us."[14] We are on a common journey, often avoiding that still voice within us, drawn away by all sorts of distractions, momentary pleasures that promise ease but leave us empty and longing for food that will last. Cultivating my deeper desires invites me to slow down enough to hear the voice within. I am called to be present to what lies within me, and before me, one day at a time.

Psychological Studies on Desire

Eli Finkel, a professor of psychology at Northwestern University, in endorsing *The Psychology of Desire*, captures the wide array of desires we as human beings experience. Finkel states, "Desire can overpower us, making a mockery of our efforts to diet, to focus, to be faithful. And yet, it can make us soar, inspire invention, heroism, poetry."

Extensive research by Oishi et al on "Desires and Happiness" report that research on desire indicates that the satisfaction of low-level physical or acquired desires does not generally lead to an increase in happiness while the satisfaction of higher level desires can lead to an increase in happiness over time. "So while ideals may not always lead to happiness, they at least have the potential to contribute to it in a way that cravings do not."[15]

---

13. Palmer, *On the Brink of Everything*, 27.

14. Chittister, *Monastery of the Heart*, 11.

15. Hofmann and Nordgren, *Psychology of Desire*, 301.

We are not always aware of our deepest desires. At times, desire may start with a vague sense of dissatisfaction, discontent, and disenchantment in our life. Our world has no shortage of persons trapped in loneliness, alienation, and longing for something more. Restlessness preoccupies many persons in our world. Young people wondering about their future, others surrounded by people yet feeling all alone, and those caught in the web of compulsive and addictive patterns blinded by many false idols and desires.

Today, the number of students on university and college campuses struggling with depression, anxiety, suicidal thoughts, and psychosis across North America is rising.[16] This intensification of students' psychological needs has become a mental health crisis.

Studies suggest that 12 to 18 percent of college students are being treated for a mental disorder.[17] Six primary factors that recent research has implicated as contributing to the mental health crisis are as follows: academic pressure, financial burden, increased accessibility of higher education, increased female to male student ratio, increased use of technology, and dramatic change in the lifestyle of university and college students. All of these factors play an important role in the current mental health crisis.[18]

In one study, anxiety scores from 170 samples of American college students (representing 40,192 students) were analyzed from research conducted between 1952 to 1993. A second study looked at anxiety scores during the same years in 99 samples of children (representing 12,056 children, ages nine to seventeen). Both studies show a significantly large increase in anxiety levels, providing more evidence for what some authors have called "the age of anxiety."[19]

Why the increase in anxiety? In both studies, anxiety levels are associated with low social connectedness and high environmental threat. During the study period, social connectedness decreased because of higher divorce rates, more people living alone,

16. Gallagher, "National Survey," 12–13.

17. Flatt, "Suffering Generation," 1.

18. Flatt, "Suffering Generation."

19. Twenge, "Age of Anxiety?"

and a decline in trust in other people. Dr. Jean Twenge says many of these changes involve greater individualism, but she says there can be a downside to this: "Our greater autonomy may lead to increased challenges and excitement, but it leads to greater isolation from others, more threats to our bodies and minds, and thus higher levels of anxiety."[20]

Rabbi Kushner, in an interview on the On-Being program on NPR, highlights that "mysticism and spirituality become more attractive in periods of greater anti-religious sentiments."[21] In this world in which political, economic, and environmental crises seem to go unheeded, many young people are disillusioned with typical religious sources, which often seem disconnected from their problems if not contributing to them. So many young people I meet are not afraid of diversity and welcome inclusion of various forms. Many feel alienated from religious and political institutions fraught with scandal after scandal and yet long for more soul-satisfying desires. Some find yoga, meditation, dance, music, and friendship bonds of some comfort and peace.

In my own life, how has real change and growth come about? It seems that it usually begins with a hunger, a thirst for something more to fill the emptiness, to seek consolation amidst desolation. For many, the desire for change flows from the old adage expressed in addiction recovery circles, "being sick and tired of being sick and tired." Many of us need the price of pain to propel us forward to something better.

Models of Following One's Deeper Desires

Some well-known persons in history found notoriety from faithfully following their deeper desires, despite many hardships; people like Martin Luther King Jr., Ghandi, and Saint Francis of Assisi, to name a few. Ghandi was a skilled attorney with all the privileges that his caste society afforded him. In traveling throughout India,

20. Twenge, "Age of Anxiety?," 1007–21.
21. Tippett, "Lawrence Kushner," 29:01.

he was deeply moved by seeing firsthand the plight of so many of his poor and struggling people that he gradually desired to own less and less and died with few possessions. He followed a dream that touched his heart, the impact of which would reverberate throughout the world, inspiring millions to live simply and work for justice, nonviolence, and peace. Saint Francis of Assisi, one of my real heroes, had a dream to rebuild the church, which eventually led to the founding of a Franciscan order, and a charisma that would change the world. Martin Luther King Jr., made famous by his "I Have a Dream" speech, felt compassion for the injustices he lived through as an African-American in the long struggle for civil rights, and his faith led him to a nonviolent movement for change that lives on today.

At times, this deep desire leads to fear and anxiety of the unknown. Perhaps it challenges my comfort, my own sense of autonomy and independence. If I pay attention to this desire, what will it ask of me? It is reminiscent of my own love/hate dynamic toward psychospiritual growth and change in my life. While I tend to love the outcome, I generally dread the process. This love/hate relationship with growth and change calls me to let go of a false sense of security I want to cling to and move toward being more comfortable with being uncomfortable.

Much of my early adult life was given over to desires of the more superficial kind. When clients come to me, they are longing for life changes. Like me, they have come to a point where their best efforts have left them stuck and yearning for more in life. This process of coming to reflect on and to name their desires begins the healing process. Men, in particular, are often taught that asking for help is a sign of weakness. My experience suggests that true heroes are those strong men and women who have the courage to ask for help, to be vulnerable with their true feelings. I meet regularly with a group of men who have grown to risk being vulnerable with one another, and that shared vulnerability is transformational.

You and I may have many desires at any given time. What desires take primacy and why can make all the difference. For my wife, Grace, her deeper desire was to be fully alive and to grow in love of self, others, and God. My desires, by contrast, were often much more conflicted. Oftentimes my own desire would be more for comfort, or immediate gratification. I would find a way to justify that, i.e., "I've had a busy day," or "I deserve to unwind and have a few drinks." This type of rationalization kept me self-deluded and masked my real fear and laziness and blocked me from deeper truth.

What are your obstacles or barriers to awakening to your heart's deepest longings for the call to love? Part of our human condition is the experience of alienation, where as humans we are often running from loneliness into all sorts of distractions, detours, and various compulsive or addictive patterns which block the light of holy desire. I know from my own life that fear can block us from tapping into these deeper desires. Growing up with an alcoholic parent and seeing excessive drinking embedded in my family and neighborhood culture, I followed that family pattern. Initially, it was a desire to fit in, to belong to my peers (drinking buddies), and to be free from fear and anxiety. I could only ask that cute girl to dance if I had a few drinks in me. My sports buddies and I enjoyed hanging out to drink and it was companionship. That desire, looking back, led initially to some short-lived camaraderie, but ultimately to feelings of emptiness and a feeling of being lost, confused, and further away from my deeper soul-self.

If I were to name my deeper desires then I would be called to change, but old habits would keep me locked in fear. This is the call to conversion, the call to face the real emptiness of false desires and to follow my deeper desires. How do we cultivate these deeper desires and longings? Following these deeper desires involves initially creating a spirit of openness to change. It involves slowing down, paying attention, and listening deeply. As the twentieth-century Catholic mystic Thomas Merton said, "Every moment and every event of every person's life on earth plants something in their soul."[22] But sadly, he continues, most of these seeds are lost. Here, the action may be slowing down enough to see, touch, and feel what is right before us.

22. Merton, *New Seeds Of Contemplation*, 14.

Action Plan: Some Concrete Steps to Follow One's Deepest Desires

1. *Cultivate deeper spiritual awakening:* A major barrier to growth and change in line with our deeper soul-stirrings, according to Indian Jesuit Anthony DeMello, is that most of us are asleep. Touching the deepest desires of our hearts challenges us to become awakened. My own life is deeply impacted by the twelve-step program of recovery which talks of having a gradual spiritual awakening after going through all the twelve-steps, which opens the way to a life of greater love and service versus a life run on self-will. A spiritual awakening may be sudden but more often it is a gradual process for most people that comes as a result of letting go of false attachments and desires. We can cultivate spiritual awakening by becoming teachable and open to learn from our mistakes and reach out for help.

2. *Create contemplative spaces:* Taking time for quiet reflection, meditation, and prayer, so as to create that space which allows what is close to be revealed to us. Many people find it helpful creating a regular sacred place at home where they can be still and meditate. Others find a walk or hike in nature to be a way to reconnect to the stillness of soul.

3. *Cultivate sources of support on the pathway to deeper self-discovery:* Many people find help through a variety of groups, such as self-help groups and peer groups, as well as consultation with mentors, therapists, or spiritual directors. Over this past year, I have been seeing a spiritual director and am being guided in the spiritual exercises. Saint Ignatius of Loyola developed the spiritual exercises which have helped millions of people to cultivate habits of focusing on deepest desires. It involves doing a daily examine where I reflect on my day and look at where I feel a sense of gratitude and graciousness about my encounters that day. I look at those areas that I could have reacted or responded differently, or perhaps was less selfish and more charitable or giving. I invite the spirit to

guide my actions in the day ahead, looking to grow in faith, hope, and love. This practice really works, especially if you are like me, easily distracted and swayed by tiny objects that demand my attention.

4. *Deep listening and generous listening:* Cultivated through curiosity, vulnerability, and a willingness to be present can be of great help. Thich Nhat Hanh speaks of deep listening as an awareness practice where, when we breathe deeply in mindfulness, everything becomes clear and deep.[23]

5. *Creating our eulogy rather than our resume:* In his book *The Road to Character*, David Brooks reminds us that living from our deeper desires is more about creating our eulogy than our resume.[24] Our resume is about looking good, making impressions, presenting an image or pleasing others. The other, creating a eulogy, is from the inside out, not the outside in, where character building is something to be desired in contrast to pleasing, accommodating and attaining power, prestige or status. One of the tasks I had as a chaplain in hospice was training volunteers. One assignment early on was to have them write their own obituary. While many volunteers were taken aback at first, it proved to be one of the most worthwhile of our training exercises. So many volunteers shared how the exercise led them to realize the gap between what they say they valued and how they were living their life. Isn't that true of so many of us, that the gap between our deepest values and where we place our energy may be far apart?

6. *Embracing our mortality and humbly accepting human limitations:* Saint Benedict wrote in the Rule of Life, an admonishment to his followers: "Keep your own death before your eyes each day." In writing this, Saint Benedict wasn't being morbid. He had no unhealthy fascination with death. For Saint Benedict, keeping one's death before one's eyes was all about humility, because death levels everything for us. It

23. Hanh, *Teachings on Love*, 84.

24. Brooks, *Road to Character*, xi–xii.

comes to all of us and as the old saying goes, you can't take anything with you when you're gone. This reality humbles us (or at least it should). It can help us in our learning to depend radically on God's grace alone. My hospice chaplaincy experience, and more deeply journeying with my wife through her illness and death, are powerful reminders that what is most precious and lasting is love, relationships, and living a life of meaning and integrity.

7. *Be in for the long haul:* Following our deepest desire is a lifetime journey. For Aristotle, real happiness is a final end or goal that encompasses the totality of one's life. It is not something that can be gained or lost in a few hours, like pleasurable sensations. The ultimate value of your life, as lived up to this moment, is embedded in measuring how well you have lived up to your full potential as a human being. For this reason, one cannot really make any pronouncements about whether one has lived a happy life until it is over. As Aristotle says, "for as it is not one swallow or one fine day that makes a spring, so it is not one day or a short time that makes a man blessed and happy."[25] The Greek word that usually gets translated as "happiness" is *eudaimonia,* and like most translations from ancient languages, this can be misleading. The main trouble is that happiness (especially in modern America) is often conceived of as a subjective state of mind, as when one says one is happy when one is enjoying a cool beer on a hot day, or is out "having fun" with one's friends. As I reflect on my own life, I have taken many detours, back alleys, and dead ends in that search.

25. Aristotle, *Eth. nic.* 1098a18.

Discovering the True Self

Knowing yourself is the beginning of all wisdom.

—ARISTOTLE

ONCE AWAKENED BY OUR deepest desires to heal, grow, and change, the hard work of deeper self-discovery begins. Our second pathway to psychospiritual transformation is the discovery of our true self. These concepts were introduced into psychoanalysis in 1960 by Donald Winnicott. Winnicott used the concept of the true self to describe a sense of self based on spontaneous authentic experience, and a feeling of being alive, having a real self. People in our life who have modeled an authentic life have inspired us.[1] We are not always aware of how they arrived at their authentic vocation or calling, but often they too have their stories of setbacks, detours, or struggles on that road. We, too, are called to face the psychological and/or spiritual demons within that block the more true self from emerging.

Psychospiritual barriers to one's true self have been given many names: call it ego, persona, false self, or pseudo-self, these masks keep us in hiding from our truest self. Real authentic

1. Winnicott, "Ego Distortion in Terms of True and False Self," 140–52.

growth and change demand that we face our own self-deception or false self. This false self is rooted in the fundamental lie of self-sufficiency. It is based on the lie that we can create our own destiny by our unaided will alone. There is an old adage that "ego" stands for "Edging God Out." We need a power greater than our self to mirror the light of truth rather than placing reliance solely on our own self-assessment or unaided will. The reality is that we are all capable of self-delusion.

Countless traditional self-help books promise easy guides to becoming a new person. These books are attractive because so many of us desire change, but in my experience, real change is anything but a simple process. Wilke Au and Noreen Cannon note that the process of integration of our shadow selves is a "lifetime process of knowing, healing and harmonizing our inner life."[2] They see this process as the essence of spirituality because it is our inner life that influences our perceptions, desires, thoughts, and actions. Ignoring the inner world because we do not like what we find, or postponing inner work out of fear of what we might discover, makes the shadow increasingly difficult to deal with. The longer instincts are repressed, the more hostile they become.

Thomas Merton describes this tension between being what I perceive others want or being real and authentic:

> If I do not know who I am, it is because I think I am the sort of person everyone around me wants to be. Perhaps I have never asked myself whether I really wanted to become what everybody else seems to want me to become. Perhaps if I only realized that I do not admire what everyone seems to admire, I would really begin to live after all.[3]

Do you, at times in stillness, hear a voice within calling you to slow down, to go deeper, to examine parts of your life that you have been avoiding? Looking at my own life experience, so much growth has come from pausing from myriad distractions and noise to look deeper within. Countless people who grew up in

2. Au and Cannon, *Urgings of the Heart*, 26.
3. Merton, *Seeds*, 4.

dysfunctional or addictive family systems have learned rules and roles that helped them survive. Some learn to manage the stress and conflict at home by becoming the "good child," others by becoming the one to try to make peace, and still others cope by becoming the "mascot" or making jokes. The problem is that those more rigid roles, while initially a necessary coping strategy as a child, no longer serve their growth as adults. Without help, they risk spending their lives never really discovering or embracing their true self, and so are like actors on a stage playing their role.

Relationships of true love allow us to confront the many roles and masks we use to avoid our true selves. This love is like a light breaking through the darkness of our false self. Often, that light comes through the words of others who care enough about what is truly good for us that they have the courage to confront our masks of self-deception. In twelve-step recovery parlance, this is often referred to as "tough love." I was given the precious gift of such "tough love" by a woman who was truly real, my beloved wife, Grace. She grew to know her true self through wrestling to overcome the wounds in her own family of origin. Because she was real she didn't hesitate to see and challenge falsehood, even in her spouse. To be totally honest, this was often unwelcome news for me as I was still in hiding from the truth of myself, although I would have denied it at the time.

Like many folks who also grow up in dysfunctional, alcoholic, or addictive family systems, the roots of denial and self-deception were sown in my family of origin. In my family, real feelings were rarely expressed, especially if they were painful or uncomfortable. When asked how things were going, the typical response was "great, great" and many of us really believed that was the case. Yes, conflict and negative feelings were suppressed. It mattered not if things were crashing down around me or others. This seemed to be the automatic response most often expressed. Claudia Black, therapist, author, and an expert on children of alcoholics, stated the three cardinal rules growing up in an alcoholic family are "Don't Talk, Don't Trust and Don't Feel." Such rules characterize a "closed family system" where silence, denial, rigidity, and isolation become the norm.[4]

I can vividly recall the long rides back from my parents' home in Wisconsin to Chicago, where Grace, my fiancé at the time, and I would be arguing in the car about my family's interactions or lack thereof. She could clearly see that my family had lots of issues that lay beneath the surface, but were not openly expressed or addressed. She could see that my behavior changed when I was around my family. From the outside, our family gatherings had the appearance of warmth and closeness; there was loud noise, plenty to drink, lots of chatter and laughter, but in reality, often little of real substance was shared. Problems were generally not welcome, or at least not talked about, and tensions among family members were kept under wraps and rarely spoken of. My father's drinking was clearly out of bounds to speak openly about, despite being the proverbial "elephant in the room." My wife would remark how I regressed to a more childlike state when back with my family of origin.

When my wife Grace confronted me on both my behavior and that of my family, she of course became the problem in my eyes. She was clearly not appreciating my family's Irish Catholic way of communicating. I would say, "This is how we relate, Grace, can't you see that we are close? You just don't understand Irish families." My wife was of Chinese ancestry from Taiwan. She cherished her home country of Taiwan and her Chinese ancestry. Having her own integrity, developed through years of her own painful self-discovery, she persisted. I learned over time that she was less concerned with not upsetting me, and more invested in facing reality without masks. She believed in a real way that living in the truth will set you free. I would like to say that the light of truth went on for me right away but again, it took a long time for me to come out of the dark into the light. When one is not ready to see, words of wisdom remain in the dark. It's like that old Buddhist proverb, "When the student is ready, the teacher will appear." For me to accept what my wife was saying, I would have to question

4. Black, *It Will Never Happen to Me*, 31–49.

my entire illusion of family closeness. So rather than face my discomfort, even though a part of me knew she was speaking some truth, I found it easier to criticize the messenger.

What made it even harder for me to see my true self was my deep fear of conflict. Eventually, it became harder and harder to deceive myself that my wife was exaggerating and this ultimately led to a family intervention for my father's drinking by me and my six brothers and three sisters. To my siblings' credit, once the subject was raised, most of them would acknowledge my father's drinking issues and I appreciated their courage in facing this together. Now, having worked for twenty years in the addiction recovery field, I know my experience is not dissimilar to many others who carry their own family secrets, struggles, and need for healing.

For the intervention, I contacted a close friend, a Capuchin-Franciscan priest and a recovering alcoholic himself, who did family interventions for substance abuse. This compassionate Capuchin-Franciscan priest meticulously prepared all ten of us children with meetings at my older brother's home prior to the official intervention. I vividly recall those meetings and my fear and anxiety as well as that of my six brothers and three sisters. Here we all gathered, preparing to do the unthinkable, to confront our father on his drinking and ask him to go away to substance abuse inpatient treatment, already prearranged. I lived in fear of my father's anger, as did many of my siblings growing up, which made this confronting experience so terrifying.

The interventionist asked if our mother should be present for the intervention and we all agreed that would not be good. Instinctively, we all knew that she might easily sabotage the process as a "classic enabler." We stood at the precipice of breaking through this wall of denial, built up over generations. We rehearsed like you would prepare for a play, all of us roleplaying and rehearsing our lines and scripts of what to say when it was our turn. Our words would include specific concrete memories of our Dad's drinking and how it impacted each of us personally and finally stating clearly what the consequences would be if our father did not get help. Things like, "I am here because I love you, Dad, but unless you get help, Dad, I am not going to be bringing your grandkids around anymore."

To make a long story short, the intervention was a success. My father was thrown off by the initial scene of being with the whole family under the false pretense of a "business meeting" for the family insurance agency. From his obvious first shock and look of terror, slowly he settled in enough to listen. The directive the interventionist gave my father, to "first hear your children out and then you will be able to respond at the end," really was a great help. I remember hearing my siblings sharing honestly prepared statements, my father breaking down in tears, especially after some of his daughter's sharing, and later his promise to get help and go to treatment, which he did.

I can say with gratitude that my father died nineteen years sober and that we had some very real and honest conversations, especially when he was struggling while on hospice near the end of his life. I always loved my Dad, but was so grateful to get closer to him before he died. None of this would have been possible without someone being honest about what was really happening. I am forever grateful to my wife, Grace, for her persistent courage in confronting me with the truth of our family dynamic. It would be many years later that my wife's confrontation would lead me to seek help with my own drinking problem, something I was blind to for so long. Oh, the power of self-deception! My many years spent in self-deception, holding onto a false image or persona of "a nice guy who just drank too much," almost destroyed my marriage and my life.

You see, despite being able to see my father's alcoholism, I was in real denial regarding my own excessive drinking patterns. Reflecting on this experience today, I am reminded that this same power of self-deception remains a real possibility for me at any moment, if I don't seek to practice rigorous honesty and surround myself with friends and family capable of real honesty and "tough love." There was much I discovered and continue to uncover about both the light and darkness within my soul, but I remain so grateful to be on this long journey of recovery.

I needed the help of many other good men and women to face my false self. My siblings and I discovered growth in honesty and that recovery is a "we" journey, not an "I" journey. The truth is that I was a "lost soul" suffering from a "soul-sickness," disconnected from self, others, and God. This false self kept me from hearing the harsh truth until the bottom fell out and my marriage was at risk. My wife's demands on me to seek help took great love, faith, and courage on her part. This was enough to get me to seek help but it would be some time before real change occurred.

I am more keenly aware of my tendency to self-deceive and have come to know that I desperately need God and others to remain faithful and honest to my real self. I seek help through twelve-step spirituality, counseling, and seeing a spiritual director twice monthly. Psychospiritual growth is a daily endeavor for a lifetime. One member in recovery, reflecting on his addiction to drugs and alcohol after some years of sobriety, shared, "I am so grateful that I didn't kill myself, although I had thought of doing it many times. I realize now, after these many years of sobriety that if I killed myself, I would have killed the wrong person." What this person came to realize, like so many in recovery from various addictions, is that he didn't really come to know himself until after he worked his recovery program and slowly discovered his true self. His false self was his addicted self who used alcohol and drugs to escape the truth of himself.

Spiritual Quest for the True Self

Like my own experience of denial, rationalization and self-deception, many of us live with conflicting desires and avoid facing the whole truth of ourselves. While deep down I believe there is a desire to be real, true, and free, still there remains a part of us that often runs from that. There is an old saying in Buddhism, "There is nothing more difficult than changing yourself." Thomas Merton, the twentieth-century Catholic mystic, describes the process of coming to face one's false self:

The only joy on earth is to escape from the prison of our own false self, and enter into union with the Life Who dwells within the essence of every creature and in the core of our own souls."[5]

Thich Nhat Hanh, the renowned Buddhist monk and author, says that we resist our true self to please others, as he states:

We are afraid to be ourselves, and we change who we are to be accepted. If your happiness depends entirely on the views of other people, you have no confidence in your self. Then, when you are not recognized by others as beautiful and worthy, you suffer. This is what makes you want to become something else, which is the foundation of suffering . . . True happiness and true power lies in understanding yourself, accepting yourself, having confidence in your self." Sometimes my own attachment to power, prestige and reputation can block who I am at my core identity.[6]

Henri Nouwen speaks eloquently of the search for this true identity when he entered the L'Arche community for the mentally handicapped, in an essay entitled "*My True Identity*," as he states:

The first thing that struck me when I came to live in a house with mentally handicapped people was that their liking and disliking of me had absolutely nothing to do with the many useful things I had done until then. Since nobody could read my books, the books could not impress anyone, and since most of them never went to school, my twenty years at Notre Dame, Yale, and Harvard did not provide a significant introduction. Not being able to use any of the skills that had proved so practical in the past was a real source of anxiety. I was suddenly faced with my naked self, open for affirmations and rejections, hugs and punches, smiles and tears all dependent simply on how I was perceived in the moment. In a way it seemed as though I was starting my life all over again. Relationships, connections, reputations could no longer

5. Merton, *New Seeds of Contemplation*, 25.

6. Hanh, *Art of Power*, 103.

be counted on. The experience was and, in many ways, is still the most important experience of my new life, because it forced me to discover my true identity. These broken, wounded, and completely unpretentious people forced me to let go of my relevant self—the self that can do things, show things, prove things, build things—and forced me to reclaim that unadorned self in which I am completely vulnerable, open to receive and give love regardless of any accomplishments.[7]

Getting to our true self calls for some letting go of false attachments that we cling to and perhaps feel lost without. Yet our deepest and truest self often comes when all is stripped away.

Psychological Dynamics of True Self and More Mature Self-identity

In my teaching to formators of religious communities over the past twenty years, we often explore what qualities lead to healthy psychospiritual growth. We explore human developmental processes and the importance of developing the three I's: healthy Identity, Intimacy, and Integrity throughout the lifespan. Embracing one's true self is a quest for our deepest identity (the first I) and shedding the pretense of false selves. Identity asks the questions, "Throughout my life, who am I? What is my deepest identity?" Intimacy asks "Who knows me, really?" And Integrity asks, "How do I become one person, whole and undivided?"

Developmental psychologists like Erik Erikson[8] have spoken of identity as something that absorbs a lot of energy in our teen years and young adult time. While this seems true, it is too limiting and incomplete. My experience with myself and others is that identity takes shape throughout our lives and is never really finished if we continue with that desire to become all we can be. That being said, developing a healthy sense of self-identity is crucial to healthy personality development.

7. Nouwen, *You Are the Beloved*, 37.
8. Erikson and Erikson, *Life Cycle*.

What makes for the healthy maturing person? I think it is discovering the unique person you were created to be. There is only one of you. Even identical twins can be quite different. How do you discover, embrace, and claim that core identity? What is it that blocks that self-discovery for you today? Carl Rogers, the famous psychologist who is the father of non-directive therapy, believed that the proper therapeutic environment, one that is accepting and non-judgmental, tends to move people away from self-concealment, away from being the expectations of others. The characteristic movement is where the client permits herself or himself freely to be open to the changing, fluid, process of growth. He or she then moves toward a friendly openness to what is going on within them—learning to listen sensitively to themselves. This process leads to a maximizing of real change and growth. Using Kierkegaard's more authentically satisfying terms, it means "to be that self which one truly is."[9] This is a lifelong process, never fully completed. But he also realized this path is at variance with the path usually taken and many prefer to remain in the darkness of the false self.

Many people live their whole life and never discover who they really are. They spend their life chasing someone else's vision of who they should be. Often it is the internalized parent or other authority figure that they seek acceptance from. I can recall one young man, struggling with his decision to leave a religious community, telling me that he worried about disappointing others if he chose to leave, even though in his deepest heart of hearts he was not happy or fulfilled. For him, embracing his deepest truth or identity was realizing he could no longer live out someone else's script for his life.

Who am I? Am I all the roles I play? The people I imitate? How does identity form? What stops it from developing? Erik Erikson would say that identity questions are core concerns for the young adolescent who is struggling with the tension between dependence and independence. I am my father's son or daughter but also my own person. I am with this group of peers, but also

9. Kierkegaard, *Sickness Unto Death*, 29.

my own person. Developmental growth is an ongoing series of attachments and separations. To say yes to the challenges of a new stage of life, I need to let go of the previous stage and that demands some grieving and letting go. To say yes to autonomy, I need to let go of being more dependent. Successfully navigating this initial set of hurdles happens with a good-enough sense of healthy self-esteem, whereby I generally like the person I am becoming. It happens through a series of competencies and affirmation, or where optimal gratification outweighs optimal frustration.

However, many clients over the years, along with current and former students, have shared that their sense of self feels less secure or shakier due to multiple experiences of being wounded. Wounded through bullying experiences growing up, or by not developing certain competencies such as school, art, work, sports, and the like. People with an adequate sense of identity are comfortable with themselves, their sexual identity, and adequacy. Our identity gets solidified as we grow and involves a growing appreciation of our strengths and weaknesses. People who are confused or unsure of their identity may be overly reliant on fulfilling a role and then the mask becomes the person.

Challenges of the False Self

A friend of mine in recovery received a coin that said, "To thine own self be true" and this became a life-changing mantra. This coin reminder in his pocket said to him each day, "Am I living my life to please others, to conform, or am I being authentic and true to my real self?" Discovering one's deepest identity necessitates uncovering the shadow self, pseudo-persona, or false self that we have incorporated over the years.

Obstacles to Discovering True Self

So how do we embrace this truer self? One of the first tasks is to break down the many barriers to uncover one's true self. A major obstacle here for many people is sexuality. We have for too long denied the precious gift of our bodies and in many ways have done violence to the gift of our bodies by compartmentalizing our sexuality and divorcing sexuality from our spirituality. Sex without love easily becomes a commodity to be used and discarded. Theologically, from a Christian perspective, it is a denial of the incarnation. That the Word became flesh and dwelt among us reminds us we are embodied persons. Sadly, the Christian church is still recovering from centuries-old emphasis on dualism, which saw the spirit as good and the flesh as weak. Flesh was often understood as the body. So we separated human desire from holy desire, leading many religiously-minded people to see their bodies as the enemy, the obstacle to holiness rather than its vessel. This led to a fallout, such as avoidance of feelings, especially sexual feelings and more intense shame around the body. Sexual sins were particularly egregious. This barrier exists in most other religious traditions as well.

My true self is my real self, my whole self, including my strengths and weaknesses, the grace and the wounds of my lived embodied experience. Working in the area of sexuality, I have sadly seen too often how shaming around sexuality has blocked this journey to healthy identity formation. What if the messages you received growing up said that what you thought, felt, and desired was not welcome or acceptable, especially among those you loved the most? This is often the case for many gay and lesbian people I have been privileged to journey with who fear rejection by family, friends, and church.

Another obstacle is breaking familiar habits and patterns. We are creatures of habit and the longer the habit, sometimes the harder change becomes. There is a powerful scene in the movie *The Shawshank Redemption* where a man who has been in prison for most of his life finally gets released, but has no way to live in the world outside of prison, and he ends up committing suicide. This story reminds us of the difficulties of adjusting to a reality that differs from a world that is familiar and comfortable, even if that reality is one where we are free and aligns much more with what we truly value. This is the harsh reality that change, even if preferred, is not always chosen. What in your life keeps you from changing toward what you most deeply value? One client of mine, Daniel, who died in his early twenties of alcoholism, had multiple relapses, often ending in frequent hospitalizations to the psychiatric unit of the hospital where I worked. I recall Daniel stating that he couldn't imagine ever stopping drinking because his best friends were at the tavern he frequented. When I reminded him that not one of those tavern patrons ever visited him in the hospital, he found ways to dismiss such obvious evidence. Not being able to imagine a life without alcohol, he paid the ultimate price.

Lack of self-knowledge is another obstacle to discovering our true self. The gaining of self-knowledge is the most important asceticism for all who aspire to live a spiritual life, as well as the most enduring and the most laborious. It is also the most paradoxical. When we present our surface self we can't see what is underneath because what is visible is hiding it. The self becomes known as subject, not object. Sometimes the culture seems to reward a more surface existence.

The Challenge of Addictions and Over-dependencies as Obstacles to True Self.

Bill Wilson, the cofounder of Alcoholics Anonymous, a program that has helped millions throughout the world to recover from the pain, agony, and suffering of addictions of various kinds, describes the disease of alcoholism as a "soul-sickness."[10] The psychospirituality of addiction is a spirituality of possession, where the person has no real being or is a lost soul, disconnected from self, others, and God in a profound way. Indeed, if we trace the origins of addiction, we see that the word "addicted" comes from the Latin prefix *ad*, which means "to" or "forward," and the past participle *dicere*, which means to "say" or "pronounce." This old notion meant a formal giving over or delivery by a sentence of the court, such as when surrendered to or obligated to a master.

---

10. Alcoholics Anonymous, *Twelve Steps and Twelve Traditions*, 49.

Though this more formal legal sense drops out of contemporary usage, still, the addict in a very real sense is someone who is delivered over to a master.

Gerald May, in his book *Addiction and Grace*, describes addictions and compulsions as enslavements. Psychologically, May states that addiction uses up desire, sucking life energy into specific obsessions and compulsions, leaving less energy for other people and pursuits.[11] In my work with people struggling with various addictions, I have seen firsthand the real loss of freedom as the addictive substance or behavior claims possession of their time, their thoughts, and their relationships. Clearly, they lose their sense of freedom and in a real way are claimed by the objects of their addictions. So through their own acts, addicts addict themselves, they cease to become one's own. They are left feeling restless, frightened, insecure, self-centered, anxious, and psychologically and spiritually bankrupt.

Harold Doweiko, a psychologist who has worked for many years in the addiction recovery field, has indicated that substance abuse disorders are symptoms of a spiritual disease and reminds us that the Greek word for the soul, *psyche*, is the root of the word "psychotherapy." So with regard to addiction, in a very real sense, we can speak of psychospiritual recovery from addiction as involving soul therapy. Crucial to the addiction recovery process is the integration of psychological insights into a program of recovery that fosters the person's spiritual growth.[12]

Carl Jung stated that craving for alcohol was really a search for wholeness or union with God. In a famous letter he wrote to Bill Wilson, the cofounder of Alcoholics Anonymous, he ends his letter stating, "You see, alcohol in Latin is 'spiritus' and you use the same word for the highest religious experience as well as for the most depraving poison."[13] Addictions often have been viewed in such existential and spiritual language, as Lee Jampolsky so aptly notes:

11. May, *Addiction and Grace*, 13.

12. McClone, "Psychospirituality of Addiction," 27.

13. Wilson, *Language of the Heart*, 281.

> When we look into our minds, we can see the roots of addiction. I submit that most addictive behavior stems from a three-step process of addictive thinking:
>
> 1. I am not okay the way I am. There is a void in me that needs to be filled.
> 2. There is something or someone external to myself that will fill this void.
> 3. My happiness is dependent on finding this sub-jstace, possession, or person.[14]

Compulsive use of alcohol, drugs, sex, gambling, work, or the Internet may all serve as a temporary solution to feelings of shame, loneliness, depression, or hurt feelings. However, the paradox of addictions is that the more we seek relief, the more we find misery, and the more we are fed, the more hunger we feel. The search for peace, relief, and contentment in drugs, alcohol, food, work, sex, and the Internet provides a false temporary escape that masks the real dilemma of the empty lost soul within. These disordered attachments are nonetheless attachments. They seek to fill a need or void deep within us, but ultimately leave us spiritually empty. My belief is that we cannot fully understand the road to recovery until we see that these addictions and overdependencies serve a deep need that is still unmet in the person. This need, at root, is deeply psychospiritual. The problem is that with addictions, the person often regresses to a more childlike state of maturity in this false self.

This false self has to die so that the real self can be discovered. Merton says these earthly desires we chase are shadows. Here, desire then becomes our chief satisfaction. This paradox is that by myself, I will remain lost, alone, and alienated, but by recognizing my dependence on others, I am free to fully live. The journey to my deepest self is not a series of steps or techniques, but rather an unfolding mystery of grace and wisdom freely chosen day by day. What we can do is live with a sort of psychospiritual discipline that promotes humility, detachment, and deep interiority. In other words, I seek truth, beauty, and love in each moment of life where everything depends on the quality of my acts and experience.

14. Jampolsky, "Healing the Addictive Mind," 66.

Ecumenical Sources of Spirituality and the True Self

Following my deepest desires is a spiritual quest that seeks to discover my true self and shed the many false selves that block the light of God's grace. Just as Jesus asked his followers, "Who do you say that I am?" he asks us, "Who do you say that you are? What forms your deepest identity?" As I write this, I just heard the news of the senseless tragedy by a white supremacist in New Zealand, where forty-nine men, women, and children praying at mosques were gunned down. My heart weeps at such intolerance and blindness born of ignorance. I find hope in the many efforts of dialogue such as the recent conference on Catholic and Muslim dialogue, which was created by the Vatican on Human Fraternity.[15]

The three major dimensions of Islam include beliefs, ritual practices, and the effort to improve one's character and actions. There are six major beliefs in Islam and five central practices that are referred to as the Five Pillars which lay the foundation of divine love and service to humanity.[16] Kabir Helminski notes that the spiritual psychology of Sufism is based on the distinction between the false self and the essential self.[17]

Parker Palmer reminds us that the spiritual journey is an endless process of engaging life as it is, stripping away our illusions about ourselves, our world, and the relationship of the two, moving closer to reality as we do. All forms of contemplation share the same goal to help see us through the deceptions of self and world, in order to get in touch with what Howard Thurman called "the sound of the genuine" within us and around us.[18]

Action Plan: Coming to One's True Self

1. *Honest self-examination*: Near the end of Parker Palmer's latest book entitled *On the Brink of Everything*, he provides a great

15. Francis, "Human Fraternity."
16. Hussain, *Five Pillars of Islam*.
17. Helminski, *Living Presence*, 17.
18. Palmer, *On the Brink of Everything*, 57.

summation of what coming to one's true self looks like when he says, "If we are willing to move through the gravitas of honest self-examination toward the grace of compassionate self-acceptance, the rewards are great. When we can say, I am all of the above, my shadow as well as my light, we become more at ease in our own skin, more at home on the face of the planet rich with diversity, more accepting of others who are no more or less broken—whole than we are, and better able to live as life-givers to the end of our days."[19]

2. *Listening deeply to oneself and others: Passing from sharing information to real communion.* Paul Tournier remarked that when listening deeply to a person, it is far more interesting to understand one person than to understand a hundred superficially. Tournier goes on to say that the real key is helping others to feel understood, and thereby helping the person to understand themselves better. Here we pass from information to communion.[20]

3. *Face my false self:* We can't eliminate the negative polarity, but we can shine light upon its workings. The key to the process is truth. The inner self is not an idealized self but a self without pretense, my authentic self. If I remain alienated from myself, I remain alienated from God. Am I playing a role, living out of a shadow self or persona, or am I true to myself?

4. *The search for true identity requires an honest self-love:* Love of self is not selfishness, but a humble recognition of our lives as true, good, and beautiful. Without real love of self, all other loves are distorted. I can make the mistake of either extreme, of thinking more of myself or less of myself rather than accurate self-knowledge. I often think clients who come for therapy suffer from one of these two extremes. One is being caught in shame and self-loathing or being grandiose where they think too much of themselves and are in need of ego deflation. Saint Teresa speaks of how we get stuck in

19. Palmer, *On the Brink of Everything*, 175.
20. Tournier, *Meaning of Persons*, 21–22.

thinking solely of ourselves, ironically suffering from a lack of self-knowledge.

5. *Prayer, meditation and journaling:* In twelve-step groups, prayer is often seen as our communicating with God and meditation as listening. Journaling is a disciplined practice that helps. It has many benefits such as deepening self-awareness, increasing empathy and seeing patterns of behavior, both positive and negative.

6. *Seek out guides, mentors, spiritual directors, and truth tellers:* Here the active challenge is to go inward, but we need guides, for the power of self-deception is great. I needed people in my life to keep me real and God to keep me real. Go inside, not outside. All the best therapy and spiritual direction is predicated on going deeper inside and gradually facing layers of defenses that keep the real me from emerging. In a place of nonjudgmental acceptance, I can gradually let my guard down and discover what I most deeply desire. Fears, shame, loneliness, and doubt can gradually give way to faith, hope, and love through a loving encounter, a trusting and accepting relationship.

7. *Cultivate wholehearted living:* Brene Brown, in her book *The Gifts of Imperfection,* has a chapter entitled cultivating authenticity where she says, "Authenticity is not something we have or don't have. It's a practice, a conscious choice of how we want to live."[21] She sees authenticity as the daily practice of letting go of who we think we're supposed to be and embracing who we are.

21. Brown, *Gifts of Imperfection*, 49.

PATHWAY #3

Embracing Healthy Intimacy
Growing in Love of Self, Others, and God

Love alone is capable of uniting living beings in such a way as to complete and fulfill them, for it alone takes them and joins them by what is deepest in themselves.

—Pierre Teilhard de Chardin, *The Phenomenon of Man*[1]

The fundamental law of love is expressed in all the major religious traditions. The Scriptures call us to "Love the Lord your God with all your heart and with all your soul and with all strength and with all your mind, and Love your neighbor as yourself" (Luke 10:27, NRV). Much of our need for acceptance, belonging, and oftentimes survival depends on living out of a mask or false persona. If I can be seen as lovable, acceptable, valued, then I will be truly happy. So begins the journey of the false self or persona, and as I travel this road, I move further away from the unique, precious, and beautiful gift God created me to be for the world. What would it be like if I could truly love and value myself as God created me?

1. Teilhard de Chardin, *Phenomenon of Man*, 265.

This forms the bedrock of the next pathway to psychospiritual growth, embracing healthy intimacy.

Discovering our true self implies a growth in self-discovery and self-intimacy. I can't give of myself if I don't know who I am. It involves a lifetime process of deepening my truest identity. Intimacy is a hallmark of our psychospiritual journey to deeper loving. Virginia Satir said, "The yearnings to love oneself, to love others, and to be loved by others are universal."[2]

I worked as a hospice chaplain for ten years before I became a clinical psychologist. I felt honored to hear so many stories of persons and families dealing with end of life issues. Many people would say to me, when they heard of my work in hospice, "Isn't that depressing?" After some pause, I would typically respond, "Actually, I find it really life-giving!" Over time this belief has only been reinforced. What I learned from those persons and families facing life-threatening illness is that what really matters most often rises to the surface when faced head on with our fragile mortality. People with limited time to live often have the opportunity to focus on what is essential and let go of the more superficial. They tend to be less concerned with power, position, income or image and what matters more is love, care, relationships, and faith. The challenges involve growing to embrace this new vulnerability and to take the risk of deeper loving. It is the challenge of intimacy with self, others, and the God of one's understanding. I found that after my wife died, questions of meaning, purpose, and how I spend my time moved to the forefront of my thoughts. Knowing life's fragility, relationships become hallowed ground.

The following Zen parable, entitled "True Love," speaks to this mystery of authentic loving:

> Two brothers worked together on the family farm. One was married and had a large family. The other was single. At the day's end, the brothers shared everything equally, produce and profit.
>
> Then one day the single brother said to himself, "It's not right that we should share equally the produce

2. Fjelstad, "Finding Your Deepest Yearnings," para. 3.

and the profit. I'm alone and my needs are simple." So each night he took a sack of grain from his bin and crept across the field between their houses, dumping it into his brother's bin.

Meanwhile, the married brother said to himself, "It's not right that we should share the produce and the profit equally. After all, I'm married and I have my wife and my children to look after me in years to come. My brother has no one, and no one to take care of his future." So each night he took a sack of grain and dumped it into his single brother's bin.

Both men were puzzled for years because their supply of grain never dwindled. Then one dark night the two brothers bumped into each other. Slowly it dawned on them what was happening. They dropped their sacks and embraced one another.[3]

As this Zen parable attests, the essence of true love is rooted in genuine empathy and concern for the well-being of the other. Like in the story, each brother desires the good of the other freely. Indeed, we are made for love. Despite this inner longing, we often go about our lives avoiding that which is most precious and lies right before us. This third pathway of psychospiritual growth and transformation is following our deepest inner call to love to the fullest!

Spirituality of Love and Intimacy

Most of the world's major religions speak about the call to grow in love. Thich Nhat Hanh, in his book entitled *Teachings on Love*, states, "Until we are able to love and take care of ourselves, we can not be of much help to others." He continues later by saying, "To bring about real harmony, reconciliation, and healing within, we have to understand ourselves." He suggests that looking and listening deeply, surveying our territory is the beginning of love

3. See "True Love."

meditation.[4] From the Islamic mystical tradition of Sufism we hear these words:

> "Love is like the flame of a lamp or candle. It cannot help but give light to others." —Hazrat Inayat Khan, Sufism
>
> "Love is the reality, and it is not a mere emotion. It is the great Truth that lies behind all of creation." —Rabindranath Tagore, Hinduism.[5]

As we see from the wisdom of spiritual teachers, love is something every single human is capable of embracing, giving, and receiving. And being able to practice it requires no training or special knowledge—only the realization of each of our desires to improve one another's life. Beneath everything that separates the world from itself, love holds us firm to one another. My will is often to push for my own needs, whether comfort, success, or prestige, and I end up remaining restless and lost. Today, the significance to grow in love has never been greater. The forces of hate and division, judgement and labeling echo in our world. At times it seems that the voices of love are too dim.

Psychology of Intimacy

The mystery is that often we grow and become our deepest selves less by pushing harder and more by letting go of fear and risking authentic loving. What does it mean to love deeply or to grow in intimacy from a psychology perspective? Father-son team of Dr. Thomas Malone and Dr. Patrick Malone in their book *The Art of Intimacy*, state that the outstanding quality of the intimate experience is the "sense of being in touch with our real selves." To risk self-disclosure presupposes a certain self-awareness and self-intimacy that allows me to share who I am. "Intimacy is derived from the Latin intima, meaning "inner" or 'innermost'. Your inside being is the real you, the you that only you can know . . . This sense of

---

4. Hanh, *Teachings on Love*, 21.
5. Buddha Groove, "Origins of Love," paras. 1–2.

touching our innermost core is the essence of intimacy: It contains all the qualities implied in its various definitions."[6]

Several years ago I was asked to write an article on intimacy for Human Development and Touchtone magazines. In researching this topic, what I found surprised me. First of all, I learned that, given the core elements of true intimacy, real intimacy is actually quite rare. What often presents as intimacy, often doesn't meet the acid test. Real intimacy is quite hard to come by. This is true for both women and men, but perhaps even more so for men, who may have even a harder time being more vulnerable, especially emotionally. For example, many men surveyed found it hard to name one intimate other, when given this fuller understanding of healthy intimacy. Many married men would often name their spouse or significant other; however, often that same feeling was not shared by their partner. Intimacy is hard work. Indeed, intimacy is much more complex and happens over time in a process of mutual trust and mutual vulnerability. Real love is a verb, not a noun. We don't fall in love. We choose to love and that choice is renewed daily in the choice to work at loving.

Psychologists have explored what moves people to more mature relationships of love and intimacy. In many ways this question is at the heart of much psychological research. There is no shortage of folks wanting to grow and change in their relationships. Some researchers note happiness in relationship comes more in satisfying higher-level ideals over lower-level desires that rarely lead to enduring happiness. These lower desires (cravings) are often fleeting and more focused on individual comfort over genuine concern for others.[7]

There is other research that says people change and grow in therapeutic relationships largely because of their relationship with a therapist. For example, clients who rate the therapeutic relationship highly are likely to achieve their goals in therapy. So, more significant than any particular type of therapy method or technique

---

6. Malone and Malone, Art of Intimacy, 19.

7. Hofmann and Nordgren, Psychology of Desire, 301.

is this sense of being truly valued in the therapeutic relationship.[8] So there is something about being cared for or feeling connected that helps bring about change. Growth happens in an atmosphere of acceptance, trust, openness, and love.

Carl Rogers (1902–87), a humanistic psychologist who was the father of client-centered psychotherapy, felt that for a person to "grow," they'd need an environment that provides them with genuineness (openness and self-disclosure), acceptance (being seen with unconditional positive regard), and empathy (being listened to and understood). Without these, relationships and healthy personalities will not develop as they should, much like a tree will not grow without sunlight and water.[9] Creating an atmosphere of genuine care and acceptance allows a deeper connection and can bring others to more fully embrace their true selves.

Some questions to explore in order to better understand our capacity for intimacy might be as follows: How well do I know myself with a balanced sense of my strengths and weaknesses? Do I know myself well enough to share my authentic self with others? Am I comfortable being alone with myself as well as being with others? How do I relate to women? How do I relate to men? How comfortable am I relating to those in authority? What obstacles stand in the way of my growth in healthy intimacy and affective maturity? Am I comfortable with my own sexuality and do I seek to integrate it respectfully in the commitments that I make?[10]

The first principle of love is to learn to love oneself. To me this means growing in deeper self-intimacy. Self-intimacy involves a cluster of tasks such as self-knowledge, self-acceptance, self-compassion, self-forgiveness, and self-esteem. Together, growth in these tasks leads to a deeper self-intimacy. This is not self-preoccupation or a narcissistic preoccupation with self, but a growing embrace of my strengths and limitations with the deepening knowledge that I am worthy of love and belonging. My many years of clinical experience confirm the practical research that indicates

8. Hubble et al., *Heart and Soul of Change*, 409–13.

9. Rogers, *On Becoming a Person*.

10. McClone, "Intimacy and Healthy Affective Maturity."

people have to discover and love themselves before they can surrender self and truly give of self to others.

There are countless examples of relationship problems where self-intimacy is underdeveloped, such as codependent, dominant-submissive, enmeshed, or engulfed relationships. You could add to this a whole host of possessive and addictive dynamics within relationships. Rather than two separate selves, rich in self-intimacy, these imbalanced relationships lack equality, freedom, mutuality, and reciprocity essential for true intimacy. Healthy relationships of intimacy are dynamic, evolving, and where people grow together.

Sister Anna Polcino, MD, a psychiatrist who was the former director of the House of Affirmation, an International Therapeutic Center for Clergy and Religious, edited a book on intimacy in which she highlights the importance of this self-intimacy. In the chapter on self-intimacy by Dr. Philomena Agudo, she says that, "The ability to listen to oneself is an important factor in attaining personality integration. Integration of personality involves a smooth harmonization of feelings, thoughts, and behavior."[11] So my thoughts, feelings, and actions become more real and authentic. I become less dependent on others for approval because our self-intimacy reinforces our inner sense of security. It becomes more about being myself, then needing to please.

I recall a beloved Jesuit psychiatrist mentor of mine, Father James Gill, SJ, giving me this advice when I worked with him almost twenty years ago. He would give talks all over the world to large groups of religious priests and often bishops groups on issues related to sexuality, health, and wellness. I recall just beginning to have outside workshops and presentations myself and being quite nervous about it all. I always envied Jim's calm demeanor and his appearing so at ease, giving these talks to such large groups. I once said, "Jim, you give these great talks around the world and you seem so at ease. What is your secret?" He paused, reflecting a moment, and then looked right at me and said, "Kevin, I finally came to realize that if I am not having fun, no one else will." I have never forgotten that talk and his words of wisdom. The more I reflected

11. Polcino, *Intimacy*, 17.

on this, the more I realized that what he was saying was that he grew to realize he was doing his best and to trust that was what he could control. He just does what he can, has fun doing it, and then lets go of expectations and worries less about pleasing others. I realized upon some soul-searching that I wanted everyone to like me, and my unrealistic expectations and self-centered focus blocked my freedom to enjoy and to genuinely serve others.

My wife, Grace, who taught me so much, would always say when I went to give a talk, workshop, or presentation, "Kevin, remember, it's not about you!" I eventually got the point. She was saying to prepare your best, but focus on being of service. I still need daily reminders to let go of ego and try to be present, to be of service, and to ask God and others for help. My fears around how others would receive me often became my focus early on and those loving reminders helped to center me, to try to be of service and to let my ego remain in check.

In sum, intimacy demands a more active engagement in taking the necessary risks to grow in self-intimacy and interpersonal intimacy. Healthy intimacy indeed presupposes a certain reflective self-awareness. When I interview and do psychological testing to assess candidates for entering religious life or lay formation, I always ask some questions related to their own self-awareness, such as: How well do they feel they know themselves? What do they see as their key strengths and weaknesses? Do they seem to have a healthy balance of awareness of both their unique strengths and limitations? The responses I get are enlightening as to their levels of self-understanding. For example, some immediately go to list multiple weaknesses but find it hard to name one strength, others list many strengths but avoid disclosing any acknowledgement of weakness or frailty. Those candidates with a more honest self-assessment often provide more of a balanced perspective with strengths and weaknesses. Their responses are a window to their own level of self-acceptance, self-esteem, and self-compassion.

Learning to love oneself is not easy, especially when a person feels unworthy of love and acceptance. So many clients I have worked with struggle with efforts to overcome shame. Shame is often seen as the affect of inferiority. Many describe the experience of coming to be accepted as they are when they enter various twelve-step recovery groups and realize they are not alone. Rather than feeling judged, they are welcomed with open arms and hearts from the men and women in recovery who have felt just like they did upon first seeking help. Nonjudgemental acceptance begins the slow healing process of self-acceptance and self-forgiveness. Often our motivation and desire for authentic change follows the experience of unconditional love and acceptance of others who accept us where we are. The power of the spirit that flows when we are able to share honestly from our heart is truly transformational.

Twelve-step programs like Alcoholics Anonymous, Narcotics Anonymous, Overeaters Anonymous, and Sexaholics Anonymous, among others, stress that to heal and reconcile past hurts and harms done to other persons in recovery, we must first begin by looking deeply within ourselves to our own part in the relationship breakdowns. They offer specific guidelines with the help of a sponsor to do a thorough inventory of oneself and to see where fear, resentment, ego, dishonesty, and lust drove their behavior. These twelve-step programs rooted in shared vulnerability provide the fertile ground of love, understanding, and unconditional acceptance that true love entails.

When we enjoy and value who we are becoming, we are freer to relate in less self-conscious ways with others. Psychospiritual growth and healing involves becoming less fearful of what others may think, knowing deep down that one is lovable, a person of dignity, and worthy of respect. We seek to grow, but become more fully aware that we need not have it "all together," that everyone has natural human weaknesses and limitations. Indeed grace and growth in the spiritual life often flow from embracing our imperfections rather than seeking perfection.

Developmental theorists writing on intimacy indicate that healthy adult intimacy involves the capacity to share more of one's authentic self with another. This presupposes not only a certain self-knowledge, but also skills of self-disclosure and taking the risks to share with trusted others. Communication skills can be further developed through learning how to listen well and growing in ability to empathize with others. Given the critical importance of healthy communication to growth in intimacy, how can we better understand, assess, and foster such growth in clergy, religious, or lay candidates to ministry? Parents, teachers, lovers, and friends can first model healthy communicating in their own capacity to self-disclose in appropriate ways, as well as in the way they listen, attend to, and seek to understand the other's experience.

Certain interpersonal competencies facilitate effective communication. Such competencies stress the importance of listening, empathy, and being open to the whole range of human feelings and experiences with a compassionate ear. Indeed, today there is a growing appreciation in the workplace, schools, and in ministry that affective skills and emotional intelligence skills are key to successful relationships. Gerald Arbuckle speaks of these sets of skills as having "affective competency" that allow one to achieve deeper intimacy across cultures. Arbuckle states, "People with affective competency keep sharpening their own human sensors of listening, empathy, and feeling . . . Affective competency requires hard and sometimes painful work. It involves becoming aware of one's cultural values and prejudices and how these block one's ability to listen to others."[12] In other words, it is not easy.

A central building block to intimacy is the growing capacity to trust. Having close relationships of mutual trust frees us to be more real, to let go of the need for pretense, and trust revealing our true selves. Yet many people may have real core issues with trust rooted in past relationships that left them hurt or wounded.

I can think of one male client who struggled for years from a past experience of sexual abuse and whose experience of falling in love confronted him with his long-held struggles with real intimacy. Despite his wounds, he had a deep desire to grow in love and had the courage to risk sharing these struggles in therapy. He knew that if he stayed in his fear, shame, and isolation he would not be a real partner in his relationships. Gradually, he grew to realize he could not really love another without doing the painful work

12. Arbuckle, "Cross-Cultural Pastoral Intimacy," 22.

of learning to love himself. The shame of past abuse kept him imprisoned in a wall of fear and shame, blocking his ability to trust. It took some considerable time, pain, struggle, and therapy to become vulnerable again, to trust and gradually grow in intimacy. So, embracing these deeper longings of your heart and taking the risk to reach out for help to those willing to listen and honor your story can lead to meaningful growth and change.

This is part of the mystery behind the success of many twelve-step recovery groups, where so many who felt lost, alone, and fearful found hope and trust in the support, acceptance, and shared vulnerability of other group members. Likewise, many priests have found in the context of priest support groups and other friendships the freedom to grow and deepen their own affective potential through intentional commitments of mutual support. Trust takes time to develop and involves hard work and a willingness to risk. Balanced self-care and love of others is tied to healthy love of self as reflected in the capacity for balanced self-care. Growth in healthy intimacy implies a growing capacity to care for oneself in all dimensions: body, mind, and spirit. Listening to one's needs for balance, harmony, and wholeness are key.

Sometimes drawing close to others in deeper ways comes as we more fully embrace our finite and limited nature. Facing one's mortality and facing our human limitations and, ultimately, death is no easy task, and many avoid these uncomfortable realities. To face our mortality is to know that we have limits and acceptance of these limits does not so much bring death but rather new life. I am challenged to deepen my own self-knowledge, knowledge of the other, and the capacity to communicate my authentic feelings to others, and at the same time, risk being misunderstood. The great paradox here is that by letting go and accepting our limitations, we become more alive by becoming more real. Grace and healing come through woundedness, not by seeking to avoid suffering, pain, and loss.

Patrick Collins, in his book *Intimacy*,[13] notes that fear of pain can block self-intimacy, whether that pain is from childhood or

13. Collins, *Intimacy*, 33–41.

other family of origin experiences. Many things prevent connection: unintentional drift through business and commitments; avoidance due to the fear of getting too close; inability or lack of desire to resolve conflicts that arise; prior unresolved hurtful relationships; lack of empathy; and feeling unsafe, particularly if previous disclosures are brought up as weapons in a later conversation. Many of us find that dealing with conflict is something we would rather avoid. It is often a source of discomfort and, depending on one's family of origin, could bring feelings of greater dread and panic. Yet, real connection often flows out of relationships that have been able to successfully negotiate conflict and confrontation. Most married couples discover this and often remark that moments of deepest intimacy came by working through significant marital conflicts.

Fear is probably the biggest obstacle that I hear whenever I ask people what holds them back from growing in intimacy. Fear of rejection, fear of conflict, fear of failure, and fear of being embarrassed are the most common fears. Whatever the fear, the reality is that intimacy demands the courage to risk reaching out to others in faith, and trust that one will fundamentally not be crushed in the process. Courage is born out of the conviction that ones who have learned through their mistakes are better equipped to take on the many changes and challenges they will inevitably face in their life relationships.

According to renowned psychologist Erik Erikson, intimacy with others "involves the capacity to commit" oneself to particular individuals in relationships that last over time, and the "ethical strength to abide by such commitments."[14] So, central to intimacy then are commitment, freedom, and maintaining each person's personal integrity.

Harriet Lerner in her book, *The Dance of Intimacy,* describes real intimacy as being able to express strength and vulnerability, weakness and competence in a balanced way that doesn't compromise your personal integrity.[15] In other words, a real intimate

14. Erikson, *Childhood and Society,* 263.
15. Lerner, *Dance of Intimacy,* 3.

relationship is where I am free to become my true and deepest self and the other as well. Given these definitions, who would you say is an intimate other for you?

Some others who have studied this concept of intimacy have described it in this way. For example, Wilke Au and Noreen Cannon describe intimacy as the "experience of being wholly and deeply touched by others—a mark of maturity and a fruit of the spirit."[16] All intimacy with others depends on a healthy self-intimacy. Most developmental theorists highlight this reality in different ways. In better discovering my deepest true self, the person I bring to all my relationships is more real. Self-intimacy fosters healthy adult intimacy. How can I love or draw close to another when I have failed to draw close to myself? Without a healthy, balanced understanding of my strengths and weaknesses, I bring my false self to relationships and intimacy escapes me. I may desire closeness, but I can only share who I know myself to be. All those elements are important. The task of educators, religious formators, and mentors is to help others become one person, the person God called them to be. This intimacy with self enhances our capacity for authentic intimacy with others.

Obstacles to healthy intimacy involve persons struggling to know, love, and embrace their true selves so they can be truly generative in loving without silencing, sacrificing, or betraying the self. Thich Nhat Hanh states, "To be beautiful is to be yourself."[17] He calls persons to communicate deeply first with the self. Practices such as meditation, tai chi, yoga, and prayer have been devised to cultivate inner peace and harmony. A more poignant intimacy becomes possible as two people dwell in a deep and rich stillness cultivated by these and other practices. Conversely, intimate relationships can nourish and settle us in ways that make it easier to find inner peace.

16. Au and Cannon, *Urgings of the Heart*, 115.

17. Hanh, *Art of Power*, 71.

Action Steps for Building Healthy Intimacy:

1. *Develop healthy communication skills:* Unhealthy communication can be a block to healthy intimacy and affective maturity. Communication that helps foster greater connection and communication is fundamentally a learned set of skills and behaviors built on a shared vulnerability, mutual respect, and maintaining personal integrity.

2. *Role models for healthy intimacy:* Who modeled healthy intimacy in your family, relationships, and communities? Many are challenged in this area, having grown up in families where the predominant messages led to more secrecy, denial, and avoidance of sharing real feelings. A person who is struggling to know herself or himself better has to break through these deeply ingrained messages and uncover more life-giving scripts that tell him or her it's okay to feel feelings, to express them openly, and to draw close to others in respectful ways.

3. *Facing conflict and confrontation:* Dealing effectively with conflict and confrontation are key intimacy skills and signs of growing affective maturity. People who have learned through their mistakes, trials, and errors to deal with conflict are better equipped to face the many changes and challenges they will inevitably face. Some people know their weaknesses, but lack the assertiveness to risk sharing their true feelings. They fail to assert what they want, how they feel, or deal effectively with conflict. Confrontation, without care, is control, and so when learning to confront others, we must be rooted in genuine care for the spiritual good of the other, if it is to be successful.

4. *Facing fear and other barriers to healthy intimacy:* Whenever I have done workshops on healthy intimacy, I ask participants what are their biggest barriers to growth in intimacy and the most common response is fear. It may be the fear of rejection, fear of being vulnerable, fear of embarrassment or shame, or fear of being hurt, but whatever the fear, growth demands

facing those fears head on. Intimacy is about becoming more real. Many fears of rejection are rooted in past relationship wounds. Becoming more real involves facing the shadow parts of ourselves.

5. *Embracing our limitations:* Growth in healthy intimacy challenges us to love and respect ourselves and others with our unique strengths and limitations. Here, the biggest barriers for us may be the extremes of grandiosity and inferiority. I can be blocked from intimacy because of shame, where I feel I am less than others, or grandiosity, where I feel better than others.[18]

18. McClone, "Intimacy and Healthy Affective Maturity."

PATHWAY #4

Integrity

Becoming One Whole Person

A little integrity is better than any career.
—RALPH WALDO EMERSON

PATHWAY NUMBER FOUR IS integrity. The road to joy involves grow-ing to become one whole person. The fully maturing person, grow-ing in love, is called to deepen in integrity, whole and undivided. Integrity is enhanced where the inside and outside selves match more closely together, or in a common expression, "What you see is what you get." The virtue that flows from integrity is wisdom and develops throughout our life, but often ripens more in our later years according to many developmental psychological theorists.

When my son, Matthew, was young, he loved to read and especially loved stories. A Chinese fable he especially liked was the Empty Pot Story,[1] which speaks well to this crucial theme of integrity.

The Empty Pot Story ~

1. Anonymous, *Empty Pot Story*.

By royal proclamation, the Emperor of China announced a contest to decide the next heir to the throne. The Emperor was old and had no son, and because he had been a plant-lover for years, he declared that any boy who wanted to be king should come to the palace to receive one royal seed. Whichever boy could show the best results within six months would win the contest and become the next to wear the crown.

You can imagine the excitement! Every boy in China fancied himself likely to win. Parents of boys who were talented at growing plants imagined living in splendor at the palace. On the day the seeds were to be handed out, thick crowds of hopeful boys thronged the palace. Each boy returned home with one precious possibility in his palm.

And so it was with the boy, Jun. He was already considered the best gardener in the village. His neighbors fought over the melons, bok choy, and snow peas that flourished from his garden. Anyone looking for Jun would probably find him bobbing between his rows, pulling out new weeds, moving one sapling over to catch more morning sun, transplanting another to the shade. Jun carefully carried the Emperor's seed home, sealing it securely in his hands so it wouldn't fall, but not so tightly that it might crush.

At home, he spread the bottom of a flower pot with large stones, covered the stones with pebbles, then filled the pot with rich, black, moist soil. He pressed the seed about an inch below the surface and covered it with light soil. Over the next few days Jun, along with every boy he knew and hundreds he did not know, watered his pot every day and watched for the telltale unfurling of the first leaf as it burst through the surface.

Cheun was the first boy in Jun's village to announce that his seed was sprouting through the soil, and his announcement was met with whoops of excitement and congratulations. He bragged that he would surely be the next emperor and practiced his royal skills by bossing around the younger, adoring children. Manchu was the next boy whose tiny plant had emerged from his pot, then it was Wong. Jun was puzzled—none of these boys could grow plants as well as he! But Jun's seed did not grow.

Soon sprouts emerged from pots all over the village. Boys moved their plants outside so the baby leaves could bask in the warmth of the sun. They built stone fences around their pots and zealously guarded them from mischievous children who might accidentally—or not so accidentally—topple them over. Soon, dozens of sprouts in pots throughout Jun's village were stretching out their first leaves. But Jun's seed did not grow.

He was confused with his empty pot—what was wrong? Jun carefully repotted his seed into a new pot with the very best and richest black loam from his garden. He crumbled every ball of soil into tiny particles. He gently pressed in the seed, and kept the top moist and watched the pot every day. Still Jun's seed did not grow.

Strong, powerful stalks soon emerged from the pots cared for by other boys in Jun's village. Jun was thrown into despair. The other boys laughed at him and started to mockingly say "as empty as Jun's pot" if there were no treats in their pockets, or if they had just finished their bowls of rice. Jun repotted his plant yet again, this time sprinkling dried fish throughout the soil as fertilizer. Even so, his seed did not grow.

Six months passed. The day approached when the boys were supposed to bring their plants to the palace for judging. Cheun, Manchu, Wong, and hundreds of other boys cleaned their pots till they shone, gently wiped the great leaves till the green veins glistened, and prepared themselves by dressing in their finest clothes. Some mothers or fathers walked alongside their son to hold the plant upright as he carried the pot to the palace, to keep the plant from tipping over.

"What will I do?" wailed Jun to his parents as he gazed out the window at the other boys joyfully preparing their triumphant return to the palace. "My seed wouldn't grow! My pot is empty!"

"You did the best you could," said his father, shaking his head. Added his mother, "Jun, just bring the emperor your pot, it was the best you could do."

Shame-faced, Jun carried his empty pot on the road to the palace, while gleeful boys, carrying pots tottering with huge plants, strode to his right and left.

At the palace, all the boys were lined up in rows with their blossoming plants awaiting judgment. The Emperor, wrapped in his richly embroidered silk robe, strode down the line of hopeful entrants, viewing each plant with a frown. When he came to Jun, he scowled even more and said, "What is this? You brought me an empty pot?"

It was all Jun could do to keep from crying. "If you please, Your Majesty," said Jun, "I tried my best. I planted your seed with the best soil I could find, I kept it moist and watched it every day. When the seed didn't grow I repotted it in new soil, and I even repotted it again. But it just didn't grow. I'm sorry." Jun hung his head.

"Hmm," said the Emperor. Turning so everyone could hear, he thundered, "I don't know where all these other boys got their seeds. There is no way anything could grow from the seeds we passed out for the contest, because those seeds had all been cooked!" And he smiled at Jun.

Integrity may seem to be a high price to pay, especially when others seem to be doing better, getting ahead, and having real success, yet sticking to one's principles and acting with integrity pays off ultimately as this story so powerfully depicts. What is this principle of integrity? The American Heritage Dictionary defines integrity as "a state of being unimpaired, soundness, quality or condition of being whole or undivided, steadfast adherence to a moral or ethical code." Integrity means wholeness, harmony with myself, where thinking and feeling are in sync. Integrity comes from the Latin *integer*, meaning whole, integrated, complete. Parker J. Palmer aptly states,

there are no shortcuts to wholeness. The only way to become whole is to put your arms around *everything* we know ourselves to be: self-serving and generous, spiteful and compassionate, cowardly and courageous, treacherous and trustworthy. We must be able to say to the world and to ourselves and to the world at large, "I am *all* of the above."[2]

The process of growth here demands becoming that one whole person, undivided and avoiding living compartmentally. In doing so, I grow to become more real, authentic, and shed the many masks or personas that Carl Jung spoke about. In other words, "What you see is what you get" or "To thine own self be true."

In my teaching and workshops on healthy relationships, I have come to appreciate how attention to the whole person is essential for meaningful growth. So to live fully and integrally in joy is to develop all aspects of my person, body, mind, heart, soul, and spirit. Each of these dimensions impacts the others for good or ill depending on how developed it becomes. So integrity in my physical being is where my body is reverenced as that of others. The evidence of greater integration comes in living well physically through bodily self-care, enjoyable hobbies, adequate exercise, nutrition, and rest, just to name a few.

A friend of mine shared how he has grown much more aware over the years just by learning to monitor his breathing. He said, "I notice how I am breathing, is it short, long, peaceful or rapid?" Western cultures seem to have a fragmentary view of the human body with the exception of more holistic and integrative medical models. By contrast, many Asian cultures have a more natural sensitivity to the body. Even their exercise typically is less rigorous, focusing on Tai Chi, Chi-Quon, etc., which respect the body's rhythms and are less forceful forms of working out. Many of them build skills of breathing, mindfulness, and meditation as well as good exercise. I recently had the opportunity to have some yoga sessions with my son and was keenly aware of how out of touch I have been with my body's rhythms. I found myself wanting to ask forgiveness from my body for living without awareness of its gift to me.

If my cognitive dimension is growing, then I am cultivating deeper awareness and mindfulness. I am more curious intellectually

2. Palmer, *On the Brink*, 174 (emphasis original).

and able to examine and challenge my limited perceptions and avoid dichotomous, distorted, or impulsive thought patterns. My mind gradually becomes more tolerant, less judgmental, and more open to diverse views and people. I am becoming more flexible in my thought patterns and less rigid. I grow better able to monitor my thoughts and deepen levels of mindful attention. I can more easily slow down racing thoughts, anxious thoughts, and grow to be more present in the here and now. Am I awakening consciously? Am I able to challenge negative thought patterns or other cognitive distortions? I recall one man in recovery from addiction sharing how as he felt the acceptance and love of his sponsor and the members of his twelve-step group, he felt he was becoming more tolerant and empathic. Feeling grateful for the gift of love, freely given, he grew in his compassion for others.

Unfortunately, our cognitive perceptions may often miss the mark. One friend, who had damage to her visual cortex growing up, shared with me how she learned that "I don't see what you see and you don't see what I see." Her words to me expressed what for her was the literal truth. But I kept thinking that her statement was figuratively so true as well. None of us really fully sees as another and often we may be worlds apart. So, how do we grow to a deeper awareness, understanding, and vision of one another? I have come to believe that I will always be missing something and knowing that can allow me to be more open, teachable, and avoid thinking that I will ever truly know someone completely. This includes spouses, significant others, and best friends. In this age of great polarization, it is all the more important to avoid assuming we know all about a person.

If I am developing emotionally, then emotional intelligence (EQ) becomes as important as cognitive development or IQ. It means that the affective dimensions of my life are more attended to. The goal of emotional intelligence is to grow in better identifying, expressing, and managing this wide array of feelings we have as embodied persons. The word "emote" means to move and emotions are meant to move us in certain directions. I love what Aristotle remarked when exploring emotions like anger. He said,

"Anyone can become angry, that is easy. But to become angry at the right person, at the right time and in the right way, that is not easy."[3] So, prior to modern research by Daniel Goleman[4] and others on the topic of emotional intelligence, we had this age-old wisdom from Aristotle.

If I am growing to fullness and integrity, I will have a greater emotional balance by avoiding the extremes of either being out of touch with my feelings or flooded and overwhelmed by them. Integrity with our feelings means that we will be better able to cope with the wide array of emotions that we have as embodied persons. Many emotional and relational problems end up being somatized in the body. Growing into greater integrity is to recognize that the body is a system with interrelated parts and each part affects the whole. Many people who end up in hospitals are dealing with emotional pain and stress previously not dealt with. In teaching healthy sexuality and relationships for the past twenty years, I find that the affective dimension of our sexuality is one of the most neglected. Healthy psychosexual integration often involves learning to better name and express empathy, compassion, and tenderness in relationships of love.

When clients struggle in psychotherapy, it is often because of entrenched defenses they find hard to let go of. Often, fear underlies many of these defenses. Perhaps the biggest barrier to psychospiritual growth is fear. We fear being vulnerable, we fear rejection, we fear being misunderstood, and we fear being hurt. Fear is mentioned 365 times in the bible, and I often say, "One solid fear for each day of the year." What has the power to overcome fear is love and faith. So, to grow emotionally, I am called to face my fears head on. Fear is one of the only emotions that grows by avoidance. When we run from fear, it only gets bigger.

Worry and anxiety are other emotional blocks to growth in generative love. Dr. Edward Hallowell, in his classic book on worry, provided a plan to overcome toxic worry and anxiety that involves many key steps:

3. Aristotle, *Eth. nic.* 1109a25.
4. Goleman, *Emotional Intelligence.*

Step 1: Never worry alone. A worry we share becomes more manageable.

Step 2: Get the facts. Most of what we worry about never happens. So getting the facts is to separate excess worry from realistic worry.

Step 3: Make a plan. Make concrete plans to deal with worry; if worrying about an upcoming exam, then carve out time for study, get a tutor, etc.

Step 4: Take care of yourself. This is essentially healthy self-care or getting enough rest, food, nutrition, and balance in self-care. Finally,

Step 5: Let it go! Finally, after the first four steps have been copleted and I have done all I can, then I let it go, rather than carrying the burdens of the world.[5]

My former mentor, Dr. James Gill, SJ,[6] worked for many years running therapy groups for high-powered businessmen who were told they were going to die from heart attacks if their stress levels continued. For these men, lifestyle change was truly a life or death issue. Many of these men were Type-A personalities, which meant they were easily upset over little things, often placing their health and lives at risk. What Jim did, along with Meyer Friedman, was to get these men together in a therapeutic group and help them better cope with stress. They often gave them tasks to share, such as naming what events stressed them: for example, standing in long grocery lines, fighting traffic, computer problems, etc. These are normal stressors we can all perhaps relate to, to some degree. These men's problem, however, was that they could not seem to let go, and so hung on to these various stress events all day long, and sometimes for weeks. Frustration turned into resentment, hostility, and excessive rumination. It was only after some weeks and months in therapy that these men began to see that they were the real problem. Gradually, in hearing others share their anger and

5. Hallowell, *Worry*, xxiii–xxiv.
6. Friedman et al., "Alteration of Type-A Behavior," 653–65.

resentment, they realized their own thinking and attitudes were causing severe heart issues. They could see, through witnessing each other's sharing, the devastating impact on their health and that of their peers in therapy. The study indicated that altering Type-A behavior reduces cardiac morbidity and mortality in post-infarction patients. Jim shared how these men built a bond out of their common struggle so much so that they chose to meet together for years as a group despite their formal therapy having ended.

One of my first positions as a clinical psychologist was working as a clinical director of a therapeutic day school. I learned a lot from the many students there, from ages eight to nineteen, who struggled with many emotional and or behavioral disorders. Many of these kids were highly impulsive, so when they experienced strong emotion, they often reacted with little or no thought. Part of the therapeutic training was to teach them how to slow down, stop, and think before reacting. We then trained them in a variety of alternative responses to stress, anxiety, tension, and anger without acting out. For those who were able to absorb such learning, they learned to express to staff when they were feeling "about to lose it," and perhaps take some deep breaths or draw out feelings instead. Our feelings are not the problem. In fact, feelings can be our biggest asset in relationships. The real question is what is the best way to handle this feeling that serves my deepest self and is in line with who I wish to become?

Much of our lives are lived in compartments. It takes a lot of energy to not be real. If I live divided, I am a different person in multiple areas of my life. By contrast, think of how easy it is when you share with a close friend that you trust. Knowing you are accepted as you are, and accepting yourself as you are, your sharing becomes more free and easy. Contrast that with the energy that it takes when we feel we have to play a role or wear masks in various settings.

Socially, I grow in wholeness by cultivating healthy relationships. I can begin by asking myself, "Am I growing in friendships of mutuality and reciprocity that are marked by intimacy?" "Do I have intimate friends with whom I can share deeply?" "Is mutuality, reciprocity and vulnerability part of those core relationships?" I have found that having a couple of people with whom I feel free to share honestly what I am feeling helps me to be more connected. Socially, I am more integrated if I can be myself in more and more places with the people I relate to.

The spiritual and soulful elements of life add meaning, purpose, and guide my choices and actions in line with my deepest values. I am a member of a Chicago-based Ignatian Associates group that meets monthly with a small group of people and reflects on our spiritual journey together and that helps me to stay on track. My regular twelve-step groups further help me to grow spiritually in the twelve-steps of recovery, one day at a time. The virtue that embodies integrity as we age is wisdom, often coming at the price of learning through experience and failure. Joan Chittister notes, "only those who have lived in this society long enough really stand to have the insight to know what it needs, to point out what doesn't."[7] The role of elders and wisdom figures in our life is to bring their wisdom to the decision-making table of the world, where too commonly now only pragmatism reigns.

Psychological Dynamics of Integrity

Many clients come to psychotherapy desiring to be more whole and integrated in their personal and relational lives. At times they will say, "I just don't feel right or I feel like, despite my desire to grow, I keep falling into old destructive habits." Rather than integration, they often feel various levels of disintegration which the Cambridge Dictionary defines as "becoming weaker or to be destroyed by breaking into small pieces." Indeed, some people express a feeling of being broken, fragile, and desiring to be more whole. A friend in long-term sobriety is fond of saying that for him, recovery from addiction was about "becoming one person." In his active addiction, he was living the "double life" that is so characteristic of the pre-recovery mind. Becoming whole and integrated meant

7. Chittister, *Gift of Years*, 125.

letting go of the denial, dishonesty, and further claiming his whole true self. The fifth step in recovery from addiction is rooted in the virtue of integrity where the recovering person admits to himself, God, and another human being the exact nature of their wrongs. All the energy put into denial and self-deception could now be directed to a life seeking greater truth and accountability.

Healthy personalities, in a growth model of psychology, are realistic, forward-looking, and motivated by long-range goals and plans. These people have a sense of purpose, a mission to work at accomplishing, and a reason and direction to their lives.[8] Using the pathways outlined so far, they are following their deepest desires, true self, and seeking to grow in love of self, others, and God.

Erik Erikson speaks of the psychosocial tension that deepens as we age. The integrity versus despair stage begins as the aging adult begins to tackle the problem of his or her mortality. The onset of this stage is often triggered by life events such as retirement, the loss of a spouse, the loss of friends and acquaintances, facing a terminal illness, and other changes to major roles in life. During the integrity versus despair stage, people reflect back on the life they have lived and come away with either a sense of fulfillment from a life well-lived or a sense of regret and despair over a life misspent.[9] If one is to successfully resolve this transition, they would come to a deeper sense of ego integrity. It is a sort of saying "yes" to all that has gone before with a hopeful eye to the future. If a person is growing here, they are able to look back at their life with a sense of contentment and face the end of life with a sense of wisdom and no regrets. Erikson defined this wisdom as an "informed and detached concern with life itself, even in the face of death itself."[10] Those who are unsuccessful during this phase will feel that their life has been wasted and will experience many regrets. The individual will be left with feelings of bitterness and despair. A Jungian view of personality integration seeks a more whole and undivided self where all the powers that strive will resist

---

8. Schultz, *Growth Psychology*, 20.

9. Erikson, *Childhood and Society*, 268–89.

10. Erikson and Erikson, *Life Cycle Completed*, 61.

disintegration and seek an "inner integration" rather than looking outside of oneself.[11]

Action Plan for Growing in Integrity:

1. *Walk the talk:* Integrity is a concept of consistency of actions, values, methods, measures, principles, expectations, and outcomes. Moving with greater integrity challenges us to live out of our principles. It is to live out of our deepest values or "walk the talk." What is the filter that guides my actions, as action often follows intention? Keeping your promises is one concrete way to build integrity.

2. *Practice rigorous honesty:* Indeed, honesty is one of the most important aspects of integrity. If you are dishonest or misleading with others, you become a divided self. Each lie or half-truth takes energy to maintain while blocking wholeness. When I hold back from sharing what is really going on, I move more toward playing a role, looking good, and holding back. One of the core principles of addiction recovery involves rigorous honesty. Integrity involves consistency, honesty, and truthfulness.

3. *Live in harmony and balance with our whole self:* Integrity is about becoming one person, whole and undivided. It demands a strong sense of integrity for who we have been, for who we are, and who we are becoming. We need to own and claim our whole story. There are key choices for growth, personal integrity, and individuation.

4. *Lifetime journey toward deepest self:* In sum, integrity is my lifetime journey toward wholeness and holiness by living more in line with my truest deepest self in a balanced and harmonious way. Efforts to grow love, compassion, and honesty are daily practices where we learn from both our failures and successes. While this may seem a tall order, it is a lifetime

11. Jung, *Development of Personality*, 197.

process that is never complete and never perfect, but a daily work in progress, recognizing our human limitations and vulnerabilities.

Grace Comes through the Wound

Embracing Vulnerability and Imperfection

Imperfections are not inadequacies; they are reminders that we're all in this together.

—BRENÉ BROWN

An elderly Chinese woman had two large pots. Each pot hung on the ends of a pole which she carried across her shoulders. Every day, she used this device to carry water to her home.

One of the pots was perfect and always delivered a full portion of water. The other had a deep crack in it and leaked. At the end of the long walk from the stream to the house, the cracked pot arrived only half full.

For a full two years this situation occurred daily, with the woman bringing home only one and a half pots of water. Of course, the perfect pot was proud of its accomplishments. But the poor cracked pot was ashamed of its imperfection and miserable that it could only do half of what it had been made to do.

After two years of what it perceived to be bitter failure, the cracked pot spoke to the woman one day by the stream, saying, "I am ashamed of myself because this crack in my side causes water to leak out all the way back to your house."

The old woman smiled and replied, "Did you notice that there are flowers on your side of the path, but not on the other pot's side? I have always known about your flaws, so I planted flower seeds on your side of the path, and every day while we walked back home you watered them and made them grow. For two years, I have been able to pick these beautiful flowers to decorate the table and give to my friends and neighbors. Without you being just the way you are, there would not have been this special beauty to grace our homes and lives."

Sometimes, it's the "cracks," or what we perceive as imperfections, in this reality that create something unexpected and beautiful. These "cracks" allow something to change and ultimately make the whole much richer and more interesting. Every being has its own unique purpose and destiny to fulfill. This is one of the great beauties of the Tao.[1]

Joan Chittister, in her reflections on aging, suggests that as we grow older, many discover in facing their limitations, "an opportunity to learn both humility and patience."[2]

One of the great mysteries of life is that often things fall apart before they come together. Real psychospiritual growth and transformation often come through embracing one's limitations, wounds, and hardships. Some of the most joyful people that I have encountered in my life have lived through great trials and suffering. Our limitations can be diamonds in the rough. Limitations confront us with our fragile humanity and can lead us to deeper humility as we realize our dependence on God's grace to be healed and made whole. Ronald Rolheiser describes how for many women and men around midlife, reality breaks through and we see a limited horizon at the end of the tunnel. To face this new

1. See "Ancient Story, Modern Message."
2. Chittister, *Gift of Years*, 140.

loneliness we need to see and accept the actual limits of our own lives, a pain intertwined with accepting our mortality.[3]

This reality became much more visible to me recently when I had the opportunity to hear several men with gang-related backgrounds share their stories of grace coming from the wound after spending years in prison for crimes they committed while they were teenagers. These men shared their stories of growing up, including the sufferings and wounds involved in the hardships of prison life. Such stories included surviving solitary confinement, struggles with guards and other inmates and yet finding some people along the way who treated them as people when others and the criminal justice system treated them as "subhuman." One middle-aged Latino male shared how he had been in prison for over twenty years and how one of the hardest things was adjusting to life outside prison. He shared the double challenge of being told that he couldn't be in touch with his closest brothers, who he spent time every day with in prison, when he was released. He found himself with no support on the outside. I remember him saying that, "My first day outside was worse than my worst day in prison." The first night after his release, with a small bag of belongings and letters clutched to his side, he slept on the floor of a homeless shelter, shoulder to shoulder with another homeless man. He found grace in the opportunity that some gave him for work, when most people and doors were closed. Even in deep suffering, he had the capacity to experience the grace of mercy. Pain, suffering, and loss are often the wounds that open the doorway to psychospiritual transformation. Many recovering alcoholics and addicts, as well as others facing depression and despair, are more open to experience the gift of mercy when offered. Thomas Merton notes this aptly when he states in *No Man Is an Island*:

> Only the person who has had to face despair is really convinced he needs mercy. Those who do not want mercy never seek it. It is better to find God on the threshold of despair than to risk our lives in a complacency that has never felt the need of forgiveness. A life that is without

3. Rolheiser, *Sacred Fire*, 74.

problems may literally be more hopeless than one that always verges on despair.[4]

Love is often discovered at great cost. My own experience is that real grace is often born out of loss, grief, and pain. Despite spending over ten years ministering to those people and families experiencing grief, as a hospice chaplain, I still felt ill-equipped when faced with my own experience of loss and grief. Accompanying my wife's daily battle with lymphoma, walking alongside her in her suffering and eventual death, I was often at a loss. This was a painful heart journey and a soul journey so aptly expressed by C. S. Lewis. "We can ignore even pleasure. But pain insists upon being attended to. God whispers to us in our pleasures, speaks in our conscience, but shouts in our pains: it is his megaphone to rouse a deaf world."[5] Experiencing a painful loss of a loved one confronts us with our fragile humanity and we seek to make sense of this new reality.

Life is fragile, fleeting, and each moment is precious, to be savored. I felt, and still feel, as if I am residing in two worlds simultaneously. My wife, Grace, is in many ways always with me and yet we are physically apart. This world, and the world of spirit, is seeking communion and deeper connection. One colleague, a professor at Catholic Theological Union, reminded me of the "thin veil" between this life and the world of our loved ones who have passed. Embracing our mortality allows us to treasure life and discover each moment as an opportunity to live more fully.

Psychological Dynamics

In researching for my doctorate in clinical psychology, I was exploring the work of Viktor Frankl and others to see the impact of spirituality, meaning, and purpose on coping with loss. Viktor Frankl, in his classic work *Man's Search for Meaning*,[6] shares how

---

4. Merton, *No Man Is an Island*, 21.

5. Lewis, *Problem of Pain*, 93.

6. Frankl, *Man's Search for Meaning*, 120–21.

even in the horror of Nazi concentration camps and losing most of his family in those places of death, he was able to claim that the Will to Meaning persisted and that losing so much, he could still choose how to respond. He later developed an existential form of therapy called Logotherapy that helped many find the will to meaning amidst suffering.

Many major psychological theories highlight one aspect of the mature personality, that healthy people accept limitations. Gordon Allport's model of the mature, healthy person includes embracing human frailty, knowing that he or she shares the same weaknesses.[7] One of the paradoxes of growth is that it often comes through our wounds and human limitations. There is a rapidly growing area of psychological research that deals with resiliency and post-traumatic growth to show how many people who suffer great trauma in their lives are able to not only cope but in many cases thrive in spite of their traumas. Factors that seem to be part of that experience are things like a changed perspective, motivation, and sense of meaning.

Franco's contribution through his logotherapy was to say that despite so much that we are powerless over, we can still choose how to respond, even in the worst sorts of trauma. We can discover a will to meaning. I find that after my wife's passing, I am daily becoming more keenly aware of the precious gift she has been in my life. Even in her physical absence, the love she gave remains ever fresh and has led me to feel graciousness, despite the pain of my grief. I have never been more convinced that love remains as when experiencing the legacy of her life and love amidst the bittersweet agony of my own grief.

Talking to others, including many clients in therapy who are experiencing great hardships, they seem more attuned to what matters most after experiencing a significant loss or trauma. I met an old friend that I had missed seeing for a while and we caught up. He shared how he found his life being radically changed by their day-to-day struggle with a child who struggles with depression. This friend said that what keeps him going is the many friends

7. Schultz, *Growth Psychology*, 17.

he has made, especially those who have children struggling with mental health issues and who really understand. He was unaware that my wife had passed and when I shared my grief feelings, we connected at a very real and deep level. Deep calls to deep, and shared vulnerability provides comfort and hope.

Resilience depends on supportive, responsive relationships and mastering a set of capabilities that can help us respond and adapt to adversity in healthy ways, says Shonkoff, director of the Center on the Developing Child at Harvard. "It's those capacities and relationships that can turn toxic stress into tolerable stress."[8] When confronted with the fallout of childhood trauma, why do some children adapt and overcome, while others bear lifelong scars that flatten their potential? A growing body of evidence points to one common answer: Every child who winds up doing well has had at least one stable and committed relationship with a supportive adult.

Resilience is the process of adapting well in the face of adversity, trauma, tragedy, threats, or significant sources of stress—such as family and relationship problems, serious health problems, or workplace and financial stressors. It means "bouncing back" from difficult experiences. Research has shown that resilience is ordinary, not extraordinary. People commonly demonstrate resilience. One example is the response of many Americans to the September 11, 2001 terrorist attacks and individuals' efforts to rebuild their lives. Being resilient does not mean that a person doesn't experience difficulty or distress. Emotional pain and sadness are common in people who have suffered major adversity or trauma in their lives. In fact, the road to resilience is likely to involve considerable emotional distress. Resilience is not a trait that people either have or do not have. It involves behaviors, thoughts, and actions that can be learned and developed in anyone.

There is no easy path to psychospiritual growth and transformation. "Life is difficult," as M. Scott Peck reminds us in his classic work, *The Road Less Traveled.*[9] One of the great mysteries of

8. See Walsh, "Science of Resilience," para. 3.

9. Peck, *Road Less Traveled*, 15.

life is that much psychospiritual growth and change comes about through failure. It is often true that pain is the touchstone of all progress. As a clinician, I see this time and again with clients who come to therapy harboring some sort of pain, loss, or wound that seeks healing. While it rarely feels good to be vulnerable, this is often where we need to be. It is in becoming vulnerable that we encounter the great spiritual paradox, that power is made manifest in weakness. We too are called to embrace our vulnerabilities and human imperfections to be real and transformed.

One of the greatest blocks to embracing vulnerability is shame. It is the self-rejecting of the self. It is the feeling that draws us into hiding for fear of rejection from others and that fear keeps us imprisoned in the hidden self. The walls of shame block the sunlight of transforming love and grace. I feel deeply honored by client stories of transformation and it all began with pain, loss, limitation, suffering, or some wound that sought to be healed. Sharing a problem cuts it in half.

I can recall several clients coming for psychotherapy who shared moments of grace in the midst of facing wounds of pain, loss, and grief. Whether coping with a relationship breakup, loss of a loved one, or facing wounds from one's past, grace and healing were expressed in the care of others, their own resilience or coming to a deeper compassion for others. One client faced his own life-threatening health issues and reported how he came to a deeper appreciation and gratitude for the support, love, and care of family and friends. This painful journey of mortality led to a richer embrace of daily life, work, and encounters. Another client remarked that by facing the pain in his own family of origin, he became aware that he grew more compassionate with others and was less reactive and judgmental in his relationships.

Gift of Embracing Vulnerability & Imperfection

A preacher put this question to a class of children: "If all the good people in the world were red and all the bad people in the world were green, what color would you be?" Little Linda Jean thought mightily for a moment. Then her face brightened and she replied: "Reverend, I'd be streaky!"[10] This story, taken from the *Spirituality of Imperfection*, reminds us that to be human is to be limited, fundamentally finite, and "not God." We all have weaknesses. We all make mistakes in the course of growing in love. I know that I have both loved my wife and family deeply and have also hurt them deeply. Knowing our limitations opens us up to ask for help and to be more accepting and tolerant of others' limitations. The reality is that many of us hide from our limitations and our weaknesses rather than seeing them as fundamental to who we are. I have always found it fascinating that parables of Jesus in the Scriptures so often highlight the weak, marginalized, poor, and vulnerable as open to God's grace where the righteous who pretended to be without fault were often objects of his greatest wrath.

In *Bird by Bird*, Anne Lamott cautions:

> Perfectionism is the voice of the oppressor, the enemy of the people. It will keep you cramped and insane your whole life . . . I think perfectionism is based on the obsessive belief that if you run carefully enough, hitting each stepping-stone just right, you won't have to die. The truth is that you will die anyway and that a lot of people who aren't even looking at their feet are going to do a whole lot better than you and have a lot more fun while they're doing it.[11]

Kurtz and Ketcham begin their book, *The Spirituality of Imperfection*, with this wonderful analogy from baseball. They note that we discover in our life, just like baseball, that errors are a part of the game. We see that even the best three-hundred-plus hitters strike out three times on average in the course of a game. So, to be human is to be imperfect and to deny imperfection then, is to disown oneself. A genuine spirituality is rooted in our humanity and is revealed by uncertainties, inadequacies, helplessness, and a lack of control. They explore the early Desert Fathers who were ascetics who entered the desert and encountered alienation and struggle

10. Kurtz and Ketcham, *Spirituality of Imperfection*, 56.

11. Lamott, *Bird by Bird*, 28.

that led them to face both the "good and bad angels" in each of us. As Kurtz and Ketchum so aptly state, "The very solitude of their lives as hermits led the Desert Fathers to discover that we are like others, not in our virtues and strengths, but precisely in our faults, our failings, our flaws." The acceptance of our full nature, including our capacity for good and evil, became the foundation of healing and new life.[12]

While a spirituality of imperfection seeks to accept our shortcomings as avenues to grace, perfectionism rests more on fear. It's the terror that we can't put anything into the world until it's perfect, but the extra catch is that perfectionists rarely, if ever, think anything they do is perfect. It's a way of paralyzing ourselves rather than making consistent progress and stretching ourselves. Fulfillment paradoxically comes through healthy discipline, sacrifice, and surrender. It comes not from seeking more but by being peaceful and content with less.

Psychospiritual transformation involves a radical shift in perception that begins to see self-discipline and conscious living as essential on the road to true and more lasting peace and serenity. This spiritual message has been at the heart of the world's great religious and spiritual traditions.

Pain, when not avoided or denied, is often the catalyst to deeper engagement with life.

> According to the Torah, tzuris (*tzarot* in Hebrew)—life's inevitable trials and tribulations—are part and parcel of what it means to be alive. Over thousands of years, many a Jewish commentator has remarked that our foremother sand forefathers were deeply flawed and led difficult lives. This has always been reassuring to me as I move through my own imperfect life, but I will admit that it has given me pause from time to time. If the great exemplars of our tradition were so troubled, why did God choose them as our leaders?[13]

---

12. Kurtz and Ketcham, *Spirituality of Imperfection*, 48.

13. Solomon, "Embracing Vulnerability," para. 2.

To understand that vulnerability as a strength is not easy. This is true for many men who were raised to believe they must be tough, strong and in control to be a real man. False pride can often become a wall behind which we hide from the light of God's grace. If we are caught in the prison of compulsive/addictive habits, we may be trapped in this false pride that is at the root of our denial. It is necessary to give up the search for perfection. Spirituality is less about getting it right all the time and more about realizing that pain, struggle, and mistakes are an essential part of living.

Unfortunately, perfection has lost its real meaning. The real meaning of perfection is wholeness or to be complete or whole. To be whole is to accept one's own limitations as well as strengths. James Martin puts it well when he states, "There is no perfect decision, no perfect outcome, or perfect life. Embracing imperfection helps us relax into reality. When we accept that all choices are conditional, limited, and imperfect, our lives become paradoxically more satisfying, joyful, and peaceful."[14]

Dealing with my own recovery from addictive patterns, I have learned a crucial lesson of recovery, that my weaknesses and character defects, when shared honestly to God and others, can be removed moment by moment. The steps of recovery are rooted in an honest recognition of harms done with a sincere attempt to change and grow in embracing those wounds as ways to restore broken relationships. Those recovering persons who persist in utilizing the twelve steps of recovery discover, after completing step nine of making direct amends, as the AA *Big Book* states:

> If we are painstaking about this phase of our development, we will be amazed before we are half-way through. We are going to know a new freedom and a new happiness. We will not regret the past nor wish to shut the door on it. We will comprehend the word serenity and we will know peace. No matter how far down the scale we have gone, we will see how our experience can benefit others. That feeling of uselessness and self-pity will disappear. We will lose interest in selfish things and gain

14. Martin, *Jesuit Guide*, 338.

> interest in our fellows. Self-seeking will slip away. Our whole attitude and outlook upon life will change. Fear of people and of economic insecurity will leave us. We will intuitively know how to handle situations which used to baffle us. We will suddenly realize that God is doing for us what we could not do for ourselves.[15]

This psychospiritual transformation follows working those steps and improves one's relationship with self, other, and God (Higher Power) of one's understanding. Many people who are not in twelve-step groups may experience similar transformation when they let go of control and allow others to guide them in the healing process.

I recall one client who was a teacher for over thirty years and, while a good teacher, failed to get close to his students. He was somewhat obsessive-compulsive and had an excessive need to control. His control served to keep his sexuality as a gay man hidden, even from himself. He remained in hiding regarding his own sexuality, fearing the rejection and judgement of family, colleagues, and friends. Eventually, his denial came crashing down in a depressive episode that led him to seek long-term residential treatment. At his treatment center, he felt a deep love and acceptance from his peers and from his counselors which allowed his two compartmentalized selves to come together. I can still recall his deep gratitude for his students and how he grew to be more free and present to them in his classes. He gradually let go of his excessive anxiety and need to be in control and felt free to be at home in his own skin. Making peace within, he discovered the freedom to be real with others. He said, "It was like I was seeing my students for the very first time."

Our common human weaknesses bind us together. In *The Spirituality of Imperfection*, authors Kurtz and Ketcham note that

> The message of all spirituality is that, in some mysterious way, we are all one—that therefore the joy and the sorrow of any one of us is the joy and the sorrow of all of us . . . Once we accept the common denominator of

15. Alcoholics Anonymous, *Big Book*, 83–84

our own imperfection, once we begin to put into practice the belief that imperfection is the reality we have most in common with all other people, then the defenses that deceive us begin to fall away, and we can begin to see ourselves and others as we all really are.[16]

I saw this in the men who had been released from prison and were working for a better life. They embraced their past without excuses and chose to live going forward. Spirituality is less about getting it right all the time and more about realizing that pain, struggle, and mistakes are an essential part of living.

Embracing vulnerability involves accepting our essential finite and limited humanity. It unites us with the rest of the human race when perhaps we tried to hold onto our terminal feeling of uniqueness. At the heart of the spirituality of the twelve steps is a genuine acceptance and acknowledgment of one's strengths and weaknesses. What has eluded the addict is that false notions of perfection have led to hard inner judgments, shame, and never feeling good enough. Lewis Presnall, in his classic book *The Search for Serenity*, states, "No one can be at home in his own heaven until he has learned to be at home in his own hell."[17] The full appreciation of inner serenity is achieved only after having come to terms with one's own weaknesses, limitations, and shortcomings. Indeed, the sixth and seventh steps of the twelve steps of AA deal precisely with the psychospiritual process of owning one's shortcomings and humbly asking God to remove them.

Recognizing that grace and psychospiritual growth often comes through the wound, perhaps the challenge is pursuing a spirituality that embraces imperfection, recognizes our limited humanity, and accepts vulnerability as essential for our growth. This has been reaffirmed in my years of counseling clients and realizing the connection between psychological and spiritual growth and embracing vulnerability.

Popular author and social science researcher Brené Brown reports "Getting through the 'I'm-not-good-enough'" as being an

16. Kurtz and Ketcham, *Spirituality of Imperfection*, 241–42.

17. Presnall, *Search for Serenity*, 1.

important theme in her book *The Gifts of Imperfection*. It means actively approaching life with kindness and compassion toward ourselves. Brown writes: "In cultivating compassion we draw from the wholeness of our experience—our suffering, our empathy as well as our cruelty and terror. Compassion becomes real when we recognize our shared humanity."[18] So, the heart of compassion is about accepting ourselves with our strengths and wounds.

Action Plan:

1. *Awareness:* Can I name my wounds and imperfections? In twelve-step language we speak of character defects. Being able to name and write down on paper those areas of weakness can help me to know how to embrace them more fully and ask others for help. Regular journaling, reflection and/ or daily examination can facilitate this greater awareness. As Socrates said, "the unreflective life is not worth living."

2. *Acceptance:* Accepting my human limitations as avenues for God's grace to enter in can be helpful. Accepting help and support from those who care about you and will listen to you strengthens resilience. What blocks you from accepting your weaknesses and limitations?

3. *Action:* Take active steps to be vulnerable and share with trusted others. A problem shared is a problem that becomes more manageable. The myth of self-sufficiency and unbridled competition needs to be shattered. To be human is rooted in humus, the earth, and I need to remain grounded. To do this, I need others who I can share my authentic, honest, and real self with.

4. *Social support:* Becoming active in civic groups, faith-based organizations, or other local groups provides social support and can help with reclaiming hope. Assisting others in their time of need also can benefit the helper. Embracing and

18. Brown, *Gifts of Imperfection*, 16.

accepting my limitations allows me to grow in humility to ask for help from others and from God.

5. *Shared vulnerability:* Thousands of twelve-step groups throughout the world are helping folks recover through the healing power of shared vulnerability. Cultivating connections and having good relationships with close family members, friends, or others are important in embracing our woundedness. One of the greatest lessons in my own life was recognizing how fear kept me from becoming more vulnerable and being willing to ask for help from others.

6. *Taking risks and embracing change:* We grow by being stretched and facing the transitions and sequential life challenges. So embracing change is a crucial part of living and psycho-spiritual growth. The wisdom of the serenity prayer can be a helpful guide, where we focus on distinguishing what we can change and what we cannot and the wisdom to know the difference.

7. *Nurture a positive view of yourself:* As one friend in recovery is fond of saying, "We build self-esteem through doing esteem-able acts." If you want to feel better, help others. An optimistic outlook enables you to expect that good things will happen in your life. Keeping things in perspective can help. Even when facing very painful events, try to consider the stressful situation in a broader context and keep a long-term perspective. Avoid blowing the event out of proportion. Maintain a hopeful outlook.

8. *Active self-care:* Take care of yourself. Honor your body rhythms. Engage in healthy activities that you enjoy and find relaxing. Try to exercise regularly and get enough rest.

9. *Strengthening resilience may be helpful:* For example, some people write about their deepest thoughts and feelings related to trauma or other stressful events in their lives. Meditation and spiritual practices help some people build connections and restore hope. Many become "wounded healers" where they share with others who experience similar wounds their

own experience, strength, and hope. How can my experience help others? The key is to identify ways that are likely to work well for you as part of your own personal strategy for fostering resilience.

PATHWAY #6

Simplify, Simplify

Our life is frittered away by detail . . . simplify, simplify.
—Henry David Thoreau

Thoreau's words remind us that we can easily get pulled off our path by all sorts of things that fail to satisfy. Simplifying his life allowed Thoreau a greater connection to nature, himself, and other people bringing about real growth and change. Simplifying your life is crucial to psychospiritual transformation that culminates in deeper joy. In the words of Thoreau, "I went into the woods because I wished to live deliberately, to front only the essential facts of life, and see if I could not learn what it had to teach, and not, when I came to die, discover that I had not lived."[1]

Socrates believed that the truly wise person would instinctively lead a frugal life, and he even went so far as to refuse to wear shoes. Yet, he constantly fell under the spell of the marketplace, and would go there often to look at the great variety and magnificence of the wares on display. A friend once asked him why he was so intrigued with the allure of the market. "I love to go there," Socrates replied, "to discover how many things I am perfectly

1. Thoreau, *Walden*, 87.

happy without."[2] One saying often attributed to Will Rogers humorously highlights the waste of excess. "Too many people spend money they haven't earned, to buy things they don't want, to impress people they don't like."

Many of us find ourselves clinging to various possessions fearing scarcity and end up missing what is our true abundance in treasures money can't buy. This Zen story illustrates where less is more.

> Ryokan, a Zen Master, lived the simplest kind of life in a little hut at the foot of the mountain. One evening a thief visited the hut only to discover there was nothing in it to steal.
>
> Ryokan returned and caught him. "You may have come a long way to visit me," he told the prowler, "and you should not return emptyhanded. Please take my clothes as a gift."
>
> The thief was bewildered. He took the clothes and slunk away.
>
> Ryokan sat naked, watching the moon. "Poor fellow," he mused, "I wish I could give him this beautiful moon."[3]

We need not be as dramatic as the Zen Master, but this story does remind us that our attachments to things often blind us to the precious gifts, at no cost, all around us. In her book *Soulful Simplicity*, Courtney Carver describes how living with less can lead to so much more. She says that "simplicity is more than making space in your home. It's also about creating more time in your life and more love in your heart and learning how you can be more with less."[4] Courtney has a popular blog that draws many followers young and old yearning for a simpler life. She believes that simplicity doesn't change who you are, but rather brings you back to who you are.[5]

My son and I often share how having too much "stuff" can cloud our vision of what is essential and of more lasting value.

2. Kurtz and Ketcham, *Spirituality of Imperfection*, 32

3. Archon, "10 Short Zen Stories," paras. 14–17.

4. Carver, *Soulful Simplicity*, xvii.

5. See Courtney's blog at bemorewithless.com.

Many millennials are discovering the benefits of greater simplicity, but the search for a simpler life has been a longstanding desire as the following quotes illustrate:

> Ultimate Simplicity is the glory of expression.
> —Walt Whitman

> There is no greatness where there is no simplicity, goodness and truth.
> —Leo Tolstoy

> I have just three things to teach: simplicity, patience, compassion. These three are your greatest treasures.
> —Lao Tzu

Chinese paintings are known for their simplicity. My wife, herself of Chinese ancestry, once shared with me how the beauty in Chinese paintings is because of the space in them. It's the empty space that enhances the beauty of the painting. One of my wife's mantras, my son and I learned well, was "simple and elegant." My wife never wore makeup, or wore expensive clothes, but carried herself with simplicity and elegance. She loved a bargain and often said, "Why spend hundreds of dollars when you can find something simple and elegant at a church rummage sale and then have more to donate to charity?" The joy she had in getting a cute dress or sweater at a bargain and saying, "Guess what I paid for this," was priceless! For my wife, who grew up poor, nothing should be wasted and if you live simply, others can benefit from your excess. In those simple choices, she expressed her approach to life in the words of the prophet Micah, "To do justice, and to love, kindness, and walk humbly with your God." (Mic 6:8, RSV)

David Shi, in his book *The Simple Life*, explores simple living in the history of American culture and notes in his introduction that "the simple life is almost as difficult to define as to live." While there are different understandings of the meaning of simple living, Shi notes, "Their common denominator has been the core assumption that the making of money and the accumulation of things should not be allowed to smother the purity of the soul, the life of the mind, the cohesion of the family, or the good of the commonweal." Besides being distinctively American, simple living has been a central tenet in most of the world's major religions and philosophies. Shi states, "The great spiritual teachers of the East—Zarathustra, Buddha, Lao Tse, and Confucius—all stressed that material self-control was essential to the good life and most Greek and Roman philosophers were emphatic in their praise for simple living, as were the Hebrew prophets and Jesus."[6]

Today, there is a growing interest in minimalism. Minimalism involves reducing the amount of things that clutter our lives, blocking true joy and peace. It involves becoming more mindful of what we buy, how we eat, and how we dispose of refuse, just to name a few. Decision-making is informed by a value system that honors all our planet. It is rooted in the fundamental interconnectedness of all beings. There are many reasons why minimalism is growing: Joshua Becker, best-selling author of the book *The More of Less: Finding the Life You Want under Everything You Own*, highlights ten main ones:

1. Worldwide Financial Turmoil—Many have begun living on tighter budgets. As a result, many consumers are choosing to identify the difference between essential and nonessential purchases.

2. Environmental Concern—Many people are choosing to live a minimalist life out of concern for the environment. They understand that less consumption equals less use of the earth's natural resources. And they are choosing to make a difference rather than stand idly by on the sidelines.

3. High Levels of Personal Debt—After years and years of living beyond our means, people are beginning to get the picture. Many are wisely choosing to get out from under the crushing weight of debt.

4. Increased Global Social Awareness—Injustice, poverty, and malnutrition have always existed. But as new technology has made the world smaller by making global images/news more

6. Shi, *Simple Life*, 3–4.

accessible, our awareness of the disparity has increased. Some are responding to the call and using their finances to make a difference on a global scale by feeding the hungry, providing clean drinking water, fighting back epidemics, and speaking up for the voiceless wherever it is needed.

5. Minimalist Art/Modern Aesthetics—Good art enters the soul and makes new ideas plausible. The term "minimalist art" (first used in 1929) experienced its major growth during the 1960s and 1970s, when stripping art down to its fundamental features began showing up in painting/sculpting/music. Soon, it transcended into design and architecture and began to define the term: modern design. As a result, it has entered our soul and made the idea of minimalist principles plausible as a lifestyle as well.

6. Personal Computing Advances—Personal computing advances have made minimalism far easier than ever before. Today, computers replace the need for CDs, DVDs, paper files, photo albums, calendars, calculators, books, phonebooks, notebooks, newspapers, etc.

7. The Benefits are Desired Today More than Ever—As our world continues to grow in complexity, there is far greater personal demand for many of the benefits that minimalism offers. Minimalism offers a life with less stress, less distraction, more freedom, and more time, all things that people today are desperately searching for more than ever.

8. More Online Presence—Proponents of the minimalist lifestyle are making it more accessible and attractive to others by writing about their experiences online. Bloggers such as Leo Babauta, Dave Bruno, Colin Wright, and Tammy Strobel are making it easier than ever to find advice, encouragement, and inspiration for choosing to make their living online. And many of them are choosing minimalism to make these lifestyle choices more accessible. After all, traveling the world becomes much easier when all of your belongings fit into a backpack.

9. New Lifestyles Are Available Like Never Before—The Internet is making new lifestyles possible. No longer do people have to be tied down to a typical nine-to-five job.

10. The Realization There's More to Life Than Possessions—Consumerism is alive and well. Advertisers continue to tell us that our next purchase will bring us satisfaction and people continue to believe it. But there is a growing trend of thoughtful people who are beginning to see through the falsehood and challenge this claim. They have tried finding happiness through possessions during the world's latest economic boom . . . and have been left unfulfilled.[7]

In the United States, we consume twice as much material goods as we did fifty years ago. On average, our homes contain more televisions than people. A more-with-less minimalist approach is catching on, leading to more time and energy, more money, more generosity, more freedom, less stress, less distraction, less environmental impact, and higher quality belongings.

There are many reasons that living simpler can enhance one's quality of life. For me, one of the more powerful benefits is that it is a daily reminder of focusing on the essentials over the incidentals. Essentials add meaning to my life and incidentals often get in the way. Less is often more, especially when the basic essentials are met. In the United States, despite its affluence, many people, young and old, suffer with depression, anxiety, and various forms of compulsive and addictive patterns.

In his book *Walden*, Henry David Thoreau states, "Why should we live with such hurry and waste of life? We are determined to be starved before we are hungry."[8] Simple living makes sense for so many reasons, so why is it so hard? I would say a huge part is my attachment to so many things. It is the fear of being without. What is it that you feel you cannot do without? What are you being called to let go of? Our virtue comes in being able to

7. Becker, *More of Less* (list used with permission of author). See also Becker, "10 Reasons Why Minimalism Is Growing."

8. Thoreau, *Walden*, 89.

do without rather than accumulate more. It may be physical possessions, but likely it may go deeper into letting go of all sorts of other less tangible attachments that block your ability to be truly present, available, and real in the here and now.

So fundamentally, simplicity needs to be rooted in a value system of meaning that supports this attitude on many levels, such as less is more. Freedom comes with simplicity. It is less a burden than first thought, but actually makes life lighter, easier, and clearer. It frees us up to focus on the more important things in our life. Living in simplicity will be a lifelong journey for me, and I bet for you too. Slowly, I am becoming aware of objectively gauging how I am doing, and daring to ask the questions, instead of relying on excuses of ignorance or neglect. How am I spending my time, my money, my life? Am I enjoying simple pleasures and foods? Am I using something up before buying something new? How am I enjoying God's creation in the parks and beauty of this land? Am I checking out if our library system has a book before I purchase one?

Maulana Wahiduddin Khan, in an article in *The Sunday Guardian*, December 8, 2013, wrote the following:

> The Prophet Muhammad said, "Simplicity is a part of faith." Absence of simplicity is the complex methods adopted in conducting our daily lives . . .
> It does not befit us to use this blessing for the sole achievement of our worldly material needs which in any case will be fulfilled with less effort. However, this is possible only when one makes a conscious endeavour to keep life simple.
> If we remain distracted by various trivial things of life, we will not be able to focus our minds on the higher realities of life.[9]

---

9. Khan, "Simplicity Is a Part of Faith," paras. 1, 3–4.

Psychological Dynamics of Simplicity

There is a psychology that undergirds the wisdom of simpler living. We live in a world filled with noise, clutter, and endless distractions from TV, internet, social media, and cell phones, making quiet and serene spaces harder to come by. I have had a longstanding desire for the simple life, but often find it elusive. Our lives easily become cluttered and we can lose sight of what's really important: family, friends, and peace of mind. Materialism can be an obstacle to wellness. Living a life of excess is known to create overarching feelings of depression and anxiety. It isn't just conjecture, either—there are plenty of studies that solidify the parallel between materialism and unhappiness. In particular, there is a series of studies which show that as people become more materialistic, their sense of autonomy, good relationships, and sense of purpose diminish considerably.[10]

A simple life devoid of clutter and excess gives way to a life of happiness, selflessness, and autonomy—so, for example, removing the clutter from your work area and finding that you're suddenly thinking clearer, streamlining your productivity. So many people in our world suffer from poverty, joblessness, homelessness, and economic deprivation, despite having worked hard much of their life. Add to that the countless and growing number of refugees and immigrants just trying to survive today. How can I possibly feel real empathy and compassion for them when I have never had to do without? How do I choose to live given these realities?

In recent decades, a large body of sociological and psychological research has emerged which suggests that people living high consumption lifestyles might actually decide that it is in their own immediate self-interest to consume less, irrespective of the moral arguments for reduced consumption. This research suggests that once human beings have their basic material needs satisfied, further increases in material wealth stop contributing much to our well-being. What this means is people might be able to free up time for things that really matter. Things like relationships with

---

10. Kasser et al., "Changes in Materialism."

family, friends, and pursuing one's passions, hobbies, and areas of deeper meaning.

I recall having this wonderful conversation with my son, Matthew, while on a Trappist retreat setting in Colorado for a week. He shared how he initially was not too keen on being there but after a couple days of restlessness, found himself slowing down and listening deeper within. He became energized when a Trappist friend shared an Enneagram book for him to ponder which he absorbed like a sponge. The Enneagram examines psychological and spiritual aspects of personality and he found it fun to explore his own personality type as well as his parents. Nothing like the "aha" moments of diagnosing your parents! Walking about the beautiful mountains on that trip with my wife, son, and my Trappist friend was a glorious memory etched in my soul. I wish for more such soul etchings. Simplicity feeds the soul and this sentiment has been echoed throughout history by poets, writers, and philosophers.

Action Plan:

1. *Discover your fundamental values.* Simpler living flows out of fundamental values and our personal mission in life. Robert Wicks writes that "When we know who we are (ordinariness), it is easier to determine what we should do, both in daily encounters and in life in general. It speaks of the main contribution we offer others."[11]

2. *Simplicity involves this ongoing process of distinguishing what is essential from want I may want.* Many of us getting through this trial of coronavirus have had to face these harsh realities that many poor of the world have dealt with daily over generations. Many things are desirable, but few are necessary or essential. So, work at *getting rid of things you think you need but can actually live without.* So many things we accumulate we never end up using and it just blocks our freedom.

11. Wicks, *Living a Gentle, Passionate Life*, 79.

3. *Finally get to know the poor.* Pope Francis has spoken often of having a preferential option for the poor. Our values are often shaped by who we allow into our world. I can identify with the poor by living more simply but there is no substitute for getting to know them as people and learning from them.[12] I have become more conscious of the value and motivation in simple living by spending time with those who struggle daily for life's basic necessities that I too often take for granted.

12. Martin, *Jesuit Guide*, 204.

PATHWAY #7

Embrace Solitude

We live, in fact, in a world starved for solitude, silence, and private: and therefore starved for meditation and true friendship.

—C. S. Lewis

MY FIRST PROFOUND EXPERIENCE of solitude took place when I attended my first silent retreat at a Jesuit Retreat house in Oshkosh, Wisconsin. I was a young adult and going through a deeper soul-searching period with my faith, life, and career direction. I had just experienced a painful relationship breakup, dropped out of a graduate school program in social work, and was feeling lost, alone, and questioning my future direction. I went on the retreat longing for something but not quite sure what. What I discovered on this silent retreat was that being alone left me initially more anxious, restless, and uncomfortable. I recall that, at least for the first day, it was almost unbearable and I was so restless I found it hard to sit still. But then something strange began to happen. I gradually started to look within myself and, guided by the silence and some spiritual direction, was encouraged to listen deeper within the stillness.

I can recall reflecting on my life, reading spiritual writers, and feeling drawn to a place I had so far avoided going. "Be still and know that I am God" (Ps 46:10, RSV) was one of the Scripture passages I reflected on. As time went on, the terror of that first day lessened, and by the end of the four-day retreat, I was not wanting to leave. It was like I was seeing parts of myself that I had never taken time or given space to really look at. I am so grateful for this experience in my life because it has been the spark for many more retreats since, and I no longer fear solitude but even crave it at times. Today, I carry those words of the psalmist, "Be still and know that I am God," on my car keychain to remind myself of what I can still too easily neglect. Some forty years later, that event still burns in my heart. It was like a *kairos* moment, where time stood still, and things seemed clearer, calmer, and more at peace. God comes in the stillness.

If solitude and stillness is so essential to growth, why is stillness something we tend to avoid? Thomas Merton, the Trappist monk, speaks eloquently of this problem in his book, *Thoughts in Solitude*:

> When solitude was a problem, I had no solitude. When it ceased to be a problem, I found I already possessed it, and could have possessed it all along. Yet still it was a problem because I knew after all that a merely subjective and inward solitude, the fruit of an effort at interioriza-tion, would never be enough . . . In solitude we remain face to face with the naked being of things. And yet we find that the nakedness of reality which we have feared, is neither a matter of terror nor for shame. It is clothed in the friendly communion of silence and this silence is related to love.[1]

Spiritual Reality of Solitude

Solitude can be a grace or a burden. Most of the major religious and spiritual traditions speak of the importance of creating times of solitude where one can listen to the still voice within. In his

1. Merton, *Thoughts in Solitude*, 85–86.

book *Solitude*, Anthony Storr explored the transformation process of great religious leaders as he states:

> Although enlightenments vary, the enlightenment which finally came to Buddha whilst he was meditating beneath a tree on the banks of the Niranjana river is said to have been the culmination of a long reflection on the human condition. Jesus, according to St. Matthew and St. Luke, spent forty days in the wilderness undergoing temptation by the devil before returning to proclaim his message of repentance and salvation. Mahomet, during the month of Ramadan, each year withdrew himself from the world to the cave of Hera.[2]

In the book *The Tao of Jesus*, the authors explore the topic of solitude/inwardness and state that

> Psychologically and spiritually, solitude serves as the silent matrix for self-reflection and the essential condition for the fostering of intimacy with God and others. Jesus is portrayed in the gospels as both a public figure and a seeker of solitude. Secluded mountain tops and outlying deserts were places to establish communion with the Father or to be personally tested; in either case, it was in solitude that he acquired the solace and the fortitude needed to continue his public ministry. He enjoined his disciples to do likewise. (Mk 6:31)[3]

Throughout Christian history, countless others have likewise responded to the invitation. Christian mystics have removed themselves to monasteries or cells or the tops of desert pillars. Meister Eckhart, the German mystic, cautions, however, that it is not enough to get away to the desert and that solitude is more about "detachment." So, being in an active life, if one practices detachment, one can find God in all things. Eckhart calls us to cultivate a "solitude of the spirit" when the ego abandons its illusion of self-sufficiency so as to find God shining in all things.[4]

2. Storr, *Solitude*, 34.

3. Loya et al., *Tao of Jesus*, 133.

4. Eckhart, *Bauerschmidt*, 70.

In my work, I am often asked to present workshops to groups of clergy and religious leaders on aspects of healthy relationships. I was asked to give a weeklong workshop for a group of Cistercian (Trappist) monks and Trappistine religious sisters. I learned much from these men and women contemplatives who spend most of their day in silence, prayer, and work. They shared the deep connection they were discovering between solitude and intimacy. Many of them who did honest soul-searching found that the quiet and solitude of their lives confronted them with their own pattern of self-deception and gradually led to a deeper intimacy with self, others, and God. Joan Chittister, the renowned Benedictine theologian, reminds us that "Solitude is chosen. It is the act of being alone in order to be with ourselves. We seek solitude for the sake of our soul."[5] We seek to go inward and to concentrate on the inside of us so that we can grow in compassion with others.

Solitude and the Call to our Common Humanity

We don't go into solitude to get away from people, but to draw closer to them. We connect more deeply to our fellow human beings with hearts of compassion when we explore the depths of our own being. As Chittister states, "Solitude is what forces us to assess our present as well as to review our past. Are we living now the happiest way we can in the circumstances we are in? That responsibility will be ours to the end. Solitude is what enables us to illuminate for ourselves whatever it is in us that is making it impossible."[6]

We have to come to terms with silence.

> That is the reason for choosing silence. In silence, we face and admit the gap between the depths of our being, which we consistently ignore, and the surface which is untrue to our own reality. We recognize the need to be at home with ourselves in order that we may go out to meet

5. Chittister, *Gift of Years*, 145

6. Chittister, *Gift of Years*, 147.

others, not just with a mask of affability, but with real
commitment and authentic love.[7]

I view solitude as the conscious entry into quiet for the purpose of deeper connection. To be truly alone is to be lost and feeling
alienated and disconnected, but to be in solitude is a fundamental
choice for quiet, to explore the depths that leads to deeper wisdom,
grace, and truth. Ronald Rolheiser, in his book on prayer, states
that "Solitude is a form of awareness. It's a way of being present and
perceptive within all of life. It's having a dimension of reflective-
ness in our daily lives that brings a sense of gratitude, appreciation,
peacefulness, enjoyment, and prayer. It's the sense within ordinary
life, that life is precious, sacred, and enough."[8]

Challenges We Face Embracing Solitude

James Martin, SJ, reminds us that being silent is one of the best
ways to listen to God and that silence is a part of every relationship, yet he expresses a concern that we are losing the art of silence as he states:

> We are gradually losing the art of silence. Of walking
> down the street lost in our own thoughts. Of closing
> the door to our rooms and being quiet. Of sitting on
> the park bench and just thinking. We may fear silence
> because we might fear what we might hear from the
> deepest part of ourselves. We may be afraid to hear that
> "still small" voice.[9]

Why do you find going to retreat or perhaps taking that hike
or nature walk enhances your relationships with God, self, and others? This is the story of my life. I have never had a bad experience
on retreat, especially on silent retreats. It has often led to insight,
depth, and though not always easy, has been largely fruitful. If that
turns out to be so good, why not do more? Our world is filled with

7. Merton, *Love and Living*, 41.

8. Rolheiser, *Prayer*, 2.

9. Martin, *Jesuit Guide*, 141.

people who hunger for greater soul-freedom. My own experience has taught me that God's presence is much closer than I realize, but I need to slow down to see, feel, and taste that ever-present reality. Silence and solitude brings a new solidarity with humanity.

Ronald Rolheiser, in his book *The Holy Longing*, is quick to remind us that "Solitude, as we know, is not the same thing as loneliness. It is being alone, but being alone in such a way that our very incompleteness is a source of quiet strength and not of anxious dissipation."[10] This creative silence allows me the space to confront my deeper self and life's more crucial questions as Merton states, "For we come face to face with ourselves in the lonely ground of our being, we confront many questions about the value of our existence, the reality of our commitments, the authenticity of our everyday lives."[11]

Psychological Dynamics of Solitude

Exploring the psychology embedded in solitude may help us gain further insight into how it engenders psychospiritual transformation. Donald Winnicott, the renowned psychoanalyst, has had a deep professional concern with whether a person's experience was authentic or not. Many of the patients he had learned to be over-compliant, that is, they lived in a way that others expected of them. These are patients who Winnicott felt had developed a false self, that is a self based on compliance with the wishes of others, rather than based on their own feelings. What he seems to be pointing to is something that John Bowlby pointed out; that our capacity to be alone is based on secure attachment. As Anthony Storr points out, the capacity to be alone is a valuable resource when changes of mental attitude are required. After major alterations in circumstances, a fundamental reappraisal of the significance and meaning of existence may be needed.[12]

---

10. Rolheiser, *Holy Longing*, 207–8.

11. Merton, *Love and Living*, 39.

12. Storr, *Solitude*, 18.

Storr further relates how Donald Winnicott published a paper on *The Capacity to be Alone* which has become a psychoanalytic classic. In this paper he wrote:

> It is probably true to say that in psychoanalytic literature more has been written on the fear of being alone or the wish to be alone than on the ability to be alone; also a considerable amount of work has been done on the withdrawn state, a defensive organization implying an expectation of persecution. It would seem to me that a discussion of the positive aspects of the capacity to be alone is overdo.[13]

He continues to explore how starting in infancy, our comfort and capacity to be alone in adult life is tied to the infant's experience of being comfortably alone in the presence of the mother because the child's basic needs for attachment are met and there's no need to look to the mother for anything. This is contrasted with a false life built on reactions to external stimuli. Children who learn to be overcompliant in an effort to please authority figures growing up struggle to develop this core capacity to cultivate solitude. Bowlby calls this the process of secure attachment in growing up.

Thomas Attig, in his book *How We Grieve: Relearning Our World*, notes that loss and grief of a loved one shatters our worldview and coping with this involves "relearning our world."[14] This resonates with my experience of the death of my wife, Grace, which I am still very much in the midst of working through. I too find myself living life each day walking between two worlds, and slowly discovering how to adjust and relearn this new reality without her. Entering into true solitude and avoiding the temptation of depression, isolation, or compulsive activity seems to facilitate the coping process.

Stephanie Dowrick points out that for Carl Jung, the great Swiss psychoanalyst, "solitude was a fount of healing." Dowrick notes, "There are some life-enhancing discoveries to be made

---

13. Winnicott, "Capacity to be Alone," 29.

14. Attig, *How We Grieve*, 11.

when you can face times alone with your own self."[15] There are a multitude of ways to avoid entering into the core of our being. Knowing you can enjoy your own company is a vital precursor to being able to enjoy other people's company without feelings of panic and neediness. Indeed, coming to value our own company precedes believing that one can matter to other people. Separateness and autonomy are key to healthy adult intimacy and affective maturity. I can't be together with you unless I have some sense of autonomy and separateness that I often discover in moments of solitude. Navigating solitude draws us deeper into our true self, unveiling the masks and shadow selves that only serve to block spontaneity, freedom, and authentic loving.

Mihaly Csikszentmihalyi, a psychologist who wrote *Flow: The Psychology of Optimal Experience*, explores enjoying solitude and other people. He begins his chapter on solitude by saying how several surveys by social scientists have concluded that many people claim to be most happy with friends and family or just in the company of others.[16] We are programmed to seek out the company of peers. This is not the end of the story. He says there is a long tradition of wisdom warning us that "Hell Is Other People."

The Hindu sage and Christian hermit sought peace away from the madding crowd. Many painful experiences in life involve other people. So how does one resolve this apparent contradiction? Mihaly feels that perhaps being with others is often the most meaningful and at other times exasperating experiences, especially when they go wrong. He suggests acquiring an early habit of using solitude to good advantage. He describes this process as "Taming Solitude." Mihaly examines how the way one copes with solitude makes all the difference. If being alone is seen as a chance to accomplish goals that cannot be reached in the company of others, then instead of feeling lonely, a person will enjoy solitude and might be able to learn new skills in the process. For example, I think of my process in writing this book which involved lots of hours of solitary activity and yet was energizing and growth-producing for

15. Dowrick, *Intimacy and Solitude*, 136.
16. Csikszentmihalyi, *Flow*, 165–73.

new skills of writing, reflecting, and reading more books. What counts is to set a goal, to concentrate one's psychic energy, to pay attention to the feedback, and to make certain that the challenge is appropriate to one's skill. Sooner or later the interaction will begin to hum, and the flow experience follows. Flow improves the quality of one's life and experiences.

Stephanie Dowrick explores the dynamics of solitude and reminds us that much of the problem with understanding the positive aspects of solitude is that we have tended to lump solitude/solitariness/aloneness/loneliness together. So solitude gets bad press, with many people believing that being in the company of almost anyone is preferable to being in no company at all. Stephanie states, "When we become relatively at one with our self, we are most likely to be able to welcome and take up solitude: feeling, to quote Winnicott, "calm, restful, relaxed and one with people and things when no excitement is around—whether or not you are actually alone."[17] This then leaves us less vulnerable to having someone or something fill the emptiness we are experiencing. No one person or thing will fill that void if we have not first learned to be at home with ourselves.

Action Steps:

Looking at some action steps to grow in this core principle of solitude, we can ask; What is your way of cultivating solitude?

1. *Slow down busyness:* Clearly, most people are not called to go away to a monastery, but slowing down the busyness of one's life and removing distractions can produce bountiful fruit for many.

2. *Meditation:* The word meditation comes from the Latin word *meditārī*, which has a range of meanings, including to reflect on, to study, and to practice. Christian meditation is the process of deliberately focusing on specific thoughts (such as a

17. Dowrick, *Intimacy and Solitude*, 147.

bible passage) and reflecting on their meaning in the context of the love of God.

3. *Prayer:* Prayer is a discipline and in solitude fosters deeper awareness. Ronald Rolheiser states, "How do we foster solitude? How do we get a handle on life so it doesn't just suck us through? How do we begin to lay a foundation for prayer in our lives? The first step is to put out into the deep by remaining quietly in God's presence in solitude, in silence, in prayer."[18]

4. *Make space and take retreats:* Do you ever get away to be alone with yourself in silence? What voices do you hear in that inner stillness? How does this impact your life? When was the last time you went on a retreat that lasted a day, a weekend, or even longer? Our capacity to be alone is based on secure attachment so we work to create safe space both without and within by developing greater comfort in stillness.

5. Mindfulness: Mindfulness involves cultivating a mental state achieved by focusing one's awareness on the present moment, while calmly acknowledging and accepting one's feelings, thoughts, and bodily sensations, used as a therapeutic technique. Jon Kabat-Zinn states in his book *Wherever You Go There You Are* that mindfulness "has everything to do with waking up and living in harmony with oneself and with the world. It has to do with examing who we are, with questioning our view of the world and our place in it, and with cultivating some appreciation for the fullness of each moment we are alive." Mindfulness allows us to dwell in stillness and look inward for some part of each day; we touch what is most real and reliable in ourselves and yet most easily overlooked and undervalued.[19] When we can center into ourselves, even for brief periods of time, in the face of the pull of the outer world, not having to look elsewhere for something to fill us up or make us happy, we can be at home wherever we find ourselves, at peace with things as they are, moment by moment.

18. Rolheiser, *Prayer*, 2.

19. Kabat-Zinn, *Wherever You Go There You Are*, 3.

6. *Journaling:* Journals improve mental clarity and can help solve problems and improve overall focus. If there's one thing journal writing is good for, it's clearing the mental clutter . . . Simply, whenever you have a problem and write about it in a journal, you transfer the problem from your head to the paper. I have journaled for years and it helps me to name what is going on, express gratitude, and see patterns in my life.

7 . *Connect to nature:* Whether the mountains, water, or countryside, the space and beauty nature provides helps us connect to our world, ourselves and the Creator. In Storr's book *Solitude*, he ends it with this quote from Wordsworth's "Prelude":

> When from our better selves we have too long
> Been parted by the hurrying world, and droop,
> Sick of its business, of its pleasures tired,
> How gracious, how benign is Solitude.[20]

20. Storr, *Solitude*, 202.

PATHWAY #8

Joy

Coming Home to Fullness of Life

The glory of God is the human person fully alive.

—Saint Irenaeus

My wife, Grace, embodied for me what it means to be fully alive in joy, to say "yes" to life! Her favorite quote from Saint Irenaeus, "The Glory of God is the human person fully alive," was her life's mantra. She was passionate, mindful, committed, and deeply spiritual. She felt deeply and loved fully. She embraced fully the wounds in her own family history, which were many. Despite her wounds, she remained rooted in love and integrity, knowing who she was and knowing God was her source of strength, hope, and love. I am sure that you have people in your life who in one way or another have embodied this joyful spirit of being fully alive. I view such people as precious gifts, reflective of God's active love in our lives, and they inspire us to grow in the fullness of that love.

In their book, *Passion for Life: Lifelong Psychological and Spiritual Growth*, authors Anne Brennan and Janice Brewi explore growth in generativity as essential for full life as they state, "Passion for life is passion for the fullness of life."[1] When I am able to truly see, touch, taste, smell, and hear what life unfolds before me, I am in the present moment. The precious present is about being real in the here and now, and being able to soak it in with all my bodily senses. This passion necessitates an integration of sexuality and spirituality. In their book *Holy Eros*, James and Evelyn Whitehead beautifully describe how "Eros is our desire for closeness, the visceral hope that moves us out of solitude and motivates us to chance the risky relationships of friendship and love."[2]

If we are created by love and for love, then joy and fullness of living comes in, embracing this love and passing it on. Love, in the best sense, is to desire the good for the other, as other. Our deepest joy is found in giving love to others in acts of service and compassion. I have come to believe that there is something deep in each human person that yearns for such life to the full. This is not a new concept but has been witnessed by many faithful guides throughout salvation history. This joy of living is about coming home to our deepest self and finding meaning and purpose for our life by seeking to live out that reality through the joys and sorrows of life.

The joy of living happens to be the theme of the twelve steps of Alcoholics Anonymous, a program of recovery that has benefited myself and millions throughout the world. As Ernest Kurtz and Katherine Ketcham note in their book *The Spirituality of Imperfection*, this joy is being welcomed home like the parable of the Prodigal Son in the Scriptures. Kurtz and Ketcham note that "Being—at home involves, first coming home to ourselves—being able to accept our own imperfect humanness. This is the first and really the only coherent meaning of another concept: self-forgiveness."[3] This requires an openness or trust that allows us to let go of fears connecting with old ideas and beliefs that we can do this by ourselves.

What makes us most human and most spiritual is recognizing that we are all connected to one another and to the world around us. We are called to be contemplatives in action and as

1. Brennan and Brewi, *Passion for Life*, 129.
2. Whitehead and Whitehead, *Holy Eros*, 10.
3. Kurtz and Ketcham, *Spirituality of Imperfection*, 232.

Saint Ignatius preached, "To find God in all things." It is a whole life of seeking greater unity in love and uniting our will with that of the Creator. Julian of Norwich, the great Christian mystic, believes that our deepest spiritual affliction is our unwillingness to believe in the absolutely unmitigated goodness of God. For Julian of Norwich, the fundamental conviction is that joy is more basic to existence than pain.

Exploring this mystery of coming to joy, we can learn from so many wisdom figures of different faiths who have gone before us, and have marked the way:

> When the mind is pure, joy follows like a shadow that
> never leaves.
> —Buddha

> Find ecstasy in life; the mere sense of living is joy
> enough.
> —Emily Dickinson

> When you do things from your soul, you feel a river
> moving in you, a joy.
> —Rumi

Life has the potential to be amazing once we concentrate on deciphering all its wonderful subtleties, nuances, and details. If we pay attention, we can find joy and ecstasy in the most simple things or in the most usual experiences. One of the richest sources of joy is getting totally immersed in an activity and putting all our soul and talent into it. The joy of creating or accomplishing something can give us an incredible boost of power.

Joy Is a Shared Experience

To get the full value of joy you must have someone to divide it with.

—MARK TWAIN

Mark Twain reminds us that joy is fundamentally a communal endeavor. Joy is one of those treasures that, paradoxically, multiplies whenever it is divided. When we share our joy, we don't lose it, but actually witness it grow stronger and wider. That happens because, just like love, joy means connection and shared happiness.

Mystical experiences are encounters with the divine or transcendent and are not relegated to only a select few. Many of us have such experiences, whether we are aware of them or not. Vernon Howard, in *The Mystic Path to Cosmic Power*, distinguishes between pseudo and authentic mysticism. Howard states, "Pseudo-mysticism seeks to evade reality; authentic mysticism wants to live it."[4] This is the road to joy! The message of mysticism for the psychospiritual journey of growth is that happiness is in the here and now by being fully present and receptive. Joyful living is a process of full engagement with life in the present moment—with all its joys, sorrows, and struggles, one day at a time.

Embracing our vulnerability and mortality invites us to live more fully in the present moment. I realized in my beloved wife's passing that she lived life to the fullest and so my memories of her remind me of the precious gift of life and not to let my moments of life pass. Life became all the more sacred and more superficial desires, while still a distraction, are surprisingly less compelling to me. I find myself wanting to surround myself with those things that matter, that last, that like true love will never die.

Archbishop Tutu was asked to consider the nature of true joy and responded, "Ultimately our greatest joy is when we seek to do good for others. It's how we are made. I mean we're wired to be compassionate. We are wired to be caring for the other and generous to one another. We shrivel when we are not able to interact."[5]

One of my clients who lives at a retirement home and has had MS (multiple sclerosis) most of her life gives me such inspiration. Although she has had to endure great pain and multiple hospitalizations through her chronic illness, she is nevertheless always expressing gratitude and spends much of her time at her retirement home playing piano and teaching other residents to experience the joy of music and song. She once told me, "Kevin, I find great joy

4. Howard, *Mystic Path*, 17.
5. Dalai Lama et al., *Book of Joy*, 59.

in seeing other residents smile and learn new songs." She said that "lifting their spirits, lifts my spirits." This is joy!

The first principle of discovering more authentic joy in living is to celebrate and taste and feel what is right in front of me. It is a matter of deep awareness, cultivating a sense of presence to what is most real and can't be measured in dollars and cents. It is saying yes to my deepest self, my truest being, and letting go of ego. In their classic work, *Presence: Human Purpose and the Field of the Future*, Peter Senge, C. Otto Schwarmer, Joseph Jaworski, and Betty Sue Flowers report how they have come to believe that the key to developing deeper levels of living fully demands true presence. Presence is the core capacity for growth and emergence with the whole. As they explored presence, they found these shifts in awareness have been recognized in spiritual traditions around the world. As they state,

> For example, in esoteric Christian traditions such shifts are associated with "grace" or "revelation" or the "Holy Spirit." Taoist theory speaks of the "transformation of the vital energy (qing) into spiritual energy (shin)." This process involves an essential quieting of the mind that Buddhists call "cessation," wherein the normal flow of thoughts ceases and the normal boundaries between self and world dissolve. In Hindu traditions, this shift is called "wholeness or oneness." In the mystic traditions of Islam, such as Sufism, it is simply known as "opening of the heart." Each tradition describes this a little differently, but all recognize it as being central to personal cultivation or maturation.[6]

Having been a hospice chaplain for ten years, I walked with hundreds of patients and families from various religious and spiritual traditions as they were facing their last days. From this sacred work, I learned that most of what matters in life becomes clearer the less time we have. At the core is faith, family, and relationships of love and compassion. The deepest desires of one's heart rise to the surface regardless of one's spiritual or religious traditions.

6. Senge et al., *Presence*, 14.

Psychological Research on Joy and Happiness

Psychological research has explored a deeper understanding of what underlies this experience of joy and happiness in life. Howard C. Cutler, MD, is a psychiatrist, New York Times best-selling author, and leading expert on the science of human happiness. Coauthor with the Dalai Lama of the internationally best-selling series *The Art of Happiness*, he summarized this research: "Today, growing scientific data confirm this insight. Researchers on human happiness identify compassionate service to others as one of the key characteristics shared by many of the world's happiest people."[7]

Previously psychology had been much more focused on pathology versus those factors that promote greater health and well-being. So rather than centering on what makes people ill, which is important, it may often be more beneficial to focus on what makes people well. Psychologists Martin Seligman and Mihaly Csikszentmihalyi helped form a framework for positive psychology which for persons is described thus: "At the individual level, it is about positive individual traits: the capacity for love and vocation, courage, interpersonal skill, aesthetic sensibility, perseverance, forgiveness, originality, future mindedness, spirituality, high talent and wisdom."[8] Why is it that some persons face enormous stress and seem to not only survive but thrive and others are crushed by life's burdens? Many of these positive traits impact how we manage stress, find joy and discover deeper meaning and purpose.

My own research as part of my doctoral program was focused on the work of Aaron Antonovsky who developed the sense of coherence scale.[9] Antonovsky developed the concept of "salutogenesis" which comes from the Latin *salus*, or "health," and the Greek *genesis*, or "origin." Antonovsky developed the term from his studies of how people manage stress and stay well and argues for seeing matters of well-being on what he calls the health ease/dis-ease continuum. As Antonovsky states, "We are all terminal cases. And

7. Cutler and Dalai Lama, *Art of Happiness*, xi.
8. Seligman and Csikszentmihali, "Positive Psychology," 5.
9. McClone, *Relationship of Core Spiritual Experiences.*

we all are, as long as there is breath of life in us, in some measure healthy. The Salutogenic orientation proposes that we study the location of each person, at any times on this continuum."[10] So a salutogenic orientation then focuses on how we promote movement to the healthy end of the continuum.

Research on authentic happiness and joy seems to be exploring what makes people live well. Such research by Frankl, Antonovsky, and others highlight how living one's life with a sense of meaning and purpose may allow persons to transform their life circumstances through positive attitudes and perspectives. The whole field of resiliency literature which has grown over these past twenty years further supports such attitudinal and spiritual factors contributing to better coping. Donald Meichenbaum, a clinical psychologist and author who has worked for over forty years with traumatized individuals writes, "Spirituality helps individuals implement their core values into social actions. Individuals who have a why to live for can bear with almost any traumatic event."[11]

Research on gratitude seems to further support that verbally expressing the gratitude we feel to people close to us helps increase and sustain our well-being above and beyond simply feeling or writing down gratitude. The world's leading expert on gratitude is Dr. Robert Emmons, a professor of psychology at the University of California, Davis. Examining the effects of writing gratitude diaries on almost two hundred college undergraduates, results showed that the gratitude group had more positive views of their life as a whole than control participants. They also reported a more positive mood and less negative mood on a daily basis during the study period.[12]

I have a regular practice of doing the Ignatian Examen which begins by reflecting on the things that I am grateful to God for that happened that day. Positive emotions can be cultivated and habituated just like negative emotions can. How do we cultivate healthy spiritual emotions such as peace, love, affection, and joy? One way

10. Antonovsky, *Unraveling the Mystery of Health*, 3–4.

11. Meichenbaum, *Roadmap to Resilience*, 163.

12. Emmons, "Why Gratitude Is Good."

seems to be through cultivating gratitude and seeing one's life in a larger perspective. Another way to cultivate positive emotion and enhance more joyful living is through sharing with others.

The Harvard longitudinal study has tracked the physical and mental health of two groups. According to its current director, Robert Waldinger, "The clearest message that we get from this 75-year study is this: Good relationships keep us happier and healthier."[13]

Scientific and neuropsychological research on our brains reminds us that feelings of limitation, anxiety, and fear are in essence habits. And habit can be unlearned. Youngey Mingyur Rinpoche explores the "biology of bliss." In his book, *The Joy of Living*, he reports how science has explored monks with years of meditation practice and training, having more objective measures of peace and happiness. As Rinopoche details:

> For example, the blood samples Richard Davidson took from the subjects of this study showed that people who demonstrated the type of prefrontal lobe activity associated with positive emotion also evidenced lower levels of cortisol, a hormone naturally produce by the adrenal glands in response to stress. Because cortisol tends to suppress the function of the immune system, some correlation can be made between feeling more or less confident, happy, and able to exert some control over one's life and having a stronger, healthier immune system, some correlation can be made between feeling more or less confident, happy and able to exert some control over one's life, and having a stronger, healthier immune system. By contrast, a general sense of being unhappy, out of control, or dependent on external circumstances tends to produce higher levels of cortisol, which in turn can weaken the immune system and make us more vulnerable to all sorts of physical diseases.[14]

Mihaly Csikszentmihalyi states that "Flow is life" and in his classic work, *Flow*, he explores the psychology of optimal experiences. One crucial aspect of optimal experiences involves

13. Curtin, "This 75-Year Harvard Study," para. 6.
14. Rinpoche, *Joy of Living*, 239.

distinguishing between pleasure and enjoyment. Real lasting peace and true joy comes through enjoyment rather than pleasure, which tends to be fleeting. Most of us grow up feeling that happiness consists of experiencing pleasure; good food, sex, and all the comforts that money can buy. We imagine traveling to exotic places and buying expensive toys. These desires, which are set by physical and social conditioning, lead to momentary satiation and relief. Mihaly notes that "pleasure, while an important component of quality of life, by itself, does not bring happiness."[15] Authentic and more lasting happiness that we may call true enjoyment goes far beyond just satisfying immediate needs or desires as he so aptly states,

> Enjoyable events occur when a person has not only met some prior expectation or satisfied a need or desire but also gone beyond what he or she has been programmed to do and achieved something unexpected, perhaps something even unimagined before.[16]

In their *Book of Joy*, Nobel Peace Prize laureates His Holiness the Dalai Lama and Archbishop Desmond Tutu share how they have come to understand the meaning of true joy. These two men knew great suffering, having experienced more than fifty years of exile and the soul-crushing violence as survivors of oppression. Despite these intense hardships, these are two of the most joyful people. Their joy is rooted in seeing life as a gift and feeling grateful their joy increases in sharing with others. They are grounded in their connectedness to all humanity, aware of their dependence on God and out of this faith they give witness to compassion, gratitude, and selfless generosity. His Holiness the Dalai Lama, responding to the Archbishop's comments on joy, shares his own reflection on the nature of true Joy:

> "As you just mentioned," the Dalai Lama added, getting quite animated, "people think about money, fame or power. From the point of view of one's own personal

15. Csikszentmihalyi, *Flow*, 46.
16. Csikszentmihalyi, *Flow*, 46.

happiness, these are short-sighted. The reality, as the Archbishop mentioned, is that human beings are social animals. One individual, no matter how powerful, how clever, cannot survive without other human beings. So, the best way to fulfill your wishes, to reach your goals, is to help others, to make more friends."[17]

The mystery of joy witnessed by these two holy men is somehow intertwined with their vision of life: that we are all part of one another and called to witness to that love which surpasses all understanding. So, like I am learning in the gradual spiritual awakening of twelve-step recovery, true joy comes in embracing our common humanity and serving others. All the previous seven pathways described prior can facilitate this lifelong journey to more lasting joy.

Action Steps:

1. *Finding your purpose:* When people discover meaning and a sense of purpose or calling they are cultivating joy. So, find creative ways to keep people happy. Help others find meaning in their life and work. Encourage them to volunteer for good causes that are meaningful for them.

2. *Cultivate a habit of identifying and expressing gratitude:* Expressing the gratitude we feel to people close to us helps increase and sustain our well-being above and beyond simply feeling or writing down gratitude. Whether doing a daily Ignatius examen, or just being mindful about positive events that week, we can cultivate an attitude of gratitude. A quick and easy way to raise your happiness level is writing in a journal dedicated to things you're grateful for each day. It works every time.

3. *Develop a habit of sharing joy with others:* Relationships are the most important overall contributor to happiness. Connect to others in community. People with strong and broad

17. Dalai Lama et al., *Book of Joy*, 61.

social relationships are happier, healthier, and live longer. Close relationships with family and friends provide love, meaning, support, and increase our feelings of self-worth. Broader networks bring a sense of belonging. So, taking action to strengthen our relationships and creating new connections is essential for happiness. Joy gets multiplied in value when shared.

4. *Be of service to others:* One of the great life lessons is happiness comes in serving others. The theme of all twelve-step recovery is found in love and service. Performing random acts of kindness without expecting a reward can be another way to cultivate joy. It's unbelievable how performing small gestures for random people can bring you so much joy.

5. *Be in the present moment:* Be mindful. Really pay attention to what you're doing, consciously create your life with each purposeful action. As Thich Nhat Hanh says, "Kiss the ground with your feet when you walk." Meditate daily. Find the kind of meditation that works for you. Yoga is a moving meditation that works for me.

6. *Challenge negative thinking and promote positive thoughts:* Psychological research on depression and anxiety reminds us that negative thinking tends to be distorted and needs to be challenged in order to stop a downward spiral. There are many forms of more common distorted thinking such as all-or-none thinking, catastrophizing, and over-personalizing, which can ruin our day.

7. *Do what you love and love what you do:* Getting into flow. Do something you love every day, whether it means reading, going for a run, teaching, gardening, or a combination of a couple or a few of these things.

8. *Balanced self-care:* Take care of body, mind, and spirit. Exercise. The more intense your workout is, the happier you will be. It's scientifically proven, so go for it! Our body and our mind are connected. Being active makes us happier as well as being good for our physical health. It instantly improves our

mood and can even lift us out of a depression. We don't all need to run marathons—there are simple things we can all do to be more active each day. We can also boost our well-being by unplugging from technology, getting outside, and making sure we get enough exercise.

Conclusion

BRINGING THESE EIGHT CORE pathways together, we come home, to discover the full embrace of the transforming and merciful love of the God of our understanding into the true joy of the fullness of life. Together, these eight pathways and their practical action steps can assist in guiding us to fuller living, one day at a time. Awakened, we are cultivating our heart's deepest desires for authentic whole living leading to true transformation. When we shed these false personas and attachments we uncover more our true self. This more authentic self, in turn, draws us to become free to love more deeply. Then, gradually, with the help of others, and the higher power of our understanding, we can let go of masks of self-deception and discover more deeply who we are, who we are called to love, and how to become a more whole and integrated person. Deep calls to deep. Embracing this call to love leads to the establishment of healthy Identity, Intimacy, and Integrity, enhancing both my psychological and spiritual growth. I commit to growing in better knowing self, others, and the God of my understanding each day.

Finally, in this mystical journey, I come to discover the paradox of life, that often grace comes through the wound, and that in embracing my own vulnerability and imperfection, I grow in self-acceptance and deeper connectedness to all humanity. I am just one among many, no better, no worse. I learn that suffering, when faced honestly, need not lead to despair, but can lead me to deeper awareness, compassion, and grace. In life, errors are just part of the game. Following the pathways of solitude and simplicity allow for letting go of what is not essential and focusing on what matters most in life. In the stillness, I connect to the God within and I discover that less is more and through emptying myself, I become full. In letting go, I receive in full. The great spiritual paradox, that so many members of twelve-step programs have come to value, is that when we are able to surrender and accept our weakness and imperfections we often discover more lasting serenity. In letting go and letting God in, we discover the true joy of living, rooted in love and service to others. When love and joy enter our lives, we are called to respond, as these words of poet Mary Oliver so beautifully capture:

> If you suddenly and unexpectedly feel joy, don't hesitate. Give in to it. There are plenty of lives and whole towns destroyed or about to be. We are not wise, and not very often kind. And much can never be redeemed. Still life has some possibility left. Perhaps this is its way of fighting back, that sometimes something happens better than all the riches of power in the world. It could be anything, but very likely you notice it in the instant when love begins. Anyway, that's often the case. Anyway, whatever it is, don't be afraid of its plenty. Joy is not made to be a crumb.[1]

1. Oliver, *Swan*, 42.

Bibliography

Alcoholics Anonymous. *Big Book*. 4th ed. New York: A. A. World Services, 2001.

———. *Twelve Steps and Twelve Traditions*. New York: A. A. World Services, 1952.

Allport, G. *Pattern and Growth in Personality*. New York: Holt, Rinehart & Winston, 1961.

"Ancient Story, Modern Message: The Cracked Pot." https://www.tcmworld.org/ancient-story-modern-message-the-cracked-pot.

Antonovsky, Aaron. *Unraveling the Mystery of Health: How People Manage Stress and Stay Well*. San Francisco: Jossey-Bass, 1987.

Arbuckle, Gerald. "Cross-Cultural Pastoral Intimacy." *Human Development* 17.2 (Spring 2002) 17–22.

Archon, Sofo. "10 Short Zen Stories." *The Unbounded Spirit* (blog), n.d. https://theunboundedspirit.com/10-short-zen-stories/.

Aristotle. *The Nicomachean Ethics*. New York, Oxford University Press, 2009.

Attig, Thomas. *How We Grieve: Relearning the World*. New York: Oxford University Press, 1996.

Au, Wilke, and Noreen Cannon. *Urgings of the Heart: A Spirituality of Integration*. New York: Paulist, 1995.

Becker, Joshua. "10 Reasons Why Minimalism Is Growing." *BecomingMinimalist* (blog), n.d. https://www.becomingminimalist.com/10-reasons-why-minimalism-is-growing-a-k-a-10-reasons-you-should-adopt-the-lifestyle/.

———. *The More of Less: Finding the Life You Want under Everything You Own*. Colorado Springs: WaterBrook, 2016.

Bertoni, Steven. "The Forbes 30 Under 30 Europe List: The 3000 Top Young Leaders, Inventors and Brash Entrepreneurs." *Forbes*, January 18, 2016. https://www.forbes.com/sites/stevenbertoni/2016/01/18/meet-the-members-of-the-forbes-30-under-30-europe-list/#4bd6e8287ab9.

Black, Claudia. *It Will Never Happen To Me! Growing Up with Addiction as Youngsters, Adolescents, Adults*. Denver: MAC, 1981.

Bibliography

Brennan, Anne, and Janice Brewi. *Passion for Life: Lifelong Psychological and Spiritual Growth*. New York: Continuum, 1999.

Brooks, David. *The Road to Character*. New York: Random House, 2015.

Brown, Brené. *The Gifts of Imperfection: Let Go of Who You Think You're Supposed to be and Embrace Who You Are*. Minnesota: Hazelton. 2010.

Buddha Groove. "Origins of Love: Quotes from Spiritual Traditions." *Balance* (blog), n.d. https://blog.buddhagroove.com/origins-of-love-quotes-from-spiritual-traditions/.

Carver, Courtney. *Soulful Simplicity: How Living With Less Can Lead to so Much More*. New York: Perigee, 2017.

Casey, Michael. *Grace: On the Journey to God*. Massachusetts: Paraclete, 2018.

Chittister, Joan. *The Gift of Years: Growing Older Gracefully*. New York: Bluebridge, 2008.

————. *Monastery of the Heart: An Invitation to a Meaningful Life*. New York: Bluebridge, 2011.

Collins, Patrick. *Intimacy: And the Hungers of the Heart*. Dublin: Columbia, 1992.

Csikszentmihalyi, Mihaly. *Flow: The Psychology of Optimal Experience*. New York: Harper & Row, 1990.

Curtin, Melanie. "This 75-Year Harvard Study Found 1 Secret to Leading a Fulfilling Life." *Inc.*, February 27, 2017. https://www.inc.com/melanie-curtin/want-a-life-of-fulfillment-a-75-year-harvard-study-says-to-prioritize-this-one-t.html.

Cutler, Howard, with the Dalai Lama. *The Art of Happiness: A Guidebook for Living*. New York: Riverhead, 2009.

Dalai Lama, et al. *The Book of Joy: Lasting Happiness in a Changing World*. New York: Random House, 2016.

Dowrick, Stephanie. *Intimacy and Solitude: Balancing Closeness and Independence*. New York: Norton, 1991.

Eckhart, Meister. *Bauerschmidt: Why the Mystics Matter Now*. Notre Dame: Sorin, 2003.

Emmons, Robert. "Why Gratitude Is Good." *Greater Good*, November 16, 2010. https://greatergood.berkeley.edu/article/item/why_gratitude_is_good.

Erikson, Erik H. *Childhood and Society*. New York: Norton, 1985.

Erikson, Erik H., and Joan Erikson. *The Life Cycle Completed*. New York: Norton, 1997.

Fjelstad, Margalis. "Finding Your Deepest Yearnings." *Psychology Today*, April 28, 2014. https://www.psychologytoday.com/intl/blog/stop-caretaking-the-borderline-or-narcissist/201404/finding-your-deepest-yearnings?amp.

Flatt, Alicia Kruisselbrink. "A Suffering Generation: Six Factors Contributing to the Mental Health Crisis in North American Higher Education." *College Quarterly* 16.1 (Winter 2013).

Francis, Pope. "A Document on Human Fraternity for World Peace and Living Together." http://www.vatican.va/content/francesco/en/travels/2019/

outside/documents/papa-francesco_20190204_documento-fratellanza-umana.html.

Frankl, Viktor. *Man's Search for Meaning*. New York: Washington Square, 1959.

Friedman, Meyer, et al. "Alteration of Type A Behavior and Its Effect on Cardiac Recurrences in Post Myocardial Infarction Patients: Summary Results of the Recurrent Coronary Prevention Project." *American Heart Journal* 112.4 (1986) 653–65.

Gallagher, Robert P. "National Survey of Counseling Center Directors." http://d-scholarship.pitt.edu/28169/1/2008_National_Survey_of_Counseling_Center_Directors.pdf.

Goleman, Daniel. *Emotional Intelligence. Why It Can Matter More than IQ*. New York: Bantam, 1995.

Hallowell, Edward M. *Worry: Hope and Help for a Common Condition*. Reprint, New York: Ballantine, 2002.

Hanh, Thich Nhat. *The Art of Power*. New York: HarperOne, 1998.

———. *Teachings on Love*. New York: California Parallax, 1998.

Helminski, Kabir. *Living Presence: A Sufi Way to Mindfulness & the Essential Self*. New York: Penguin Putnam, 1992.

Hofmann, Wilhelm, and Loran F. Nordgren, eds. *The Psychology of Desire*. New York: Guilford, 2015.

Howard, Vernon. *The Mystic Path to Cosmic Power*. New York, Parker, 1967.

Hubble, Mark A., et al. *The Heart and Soul of Change: What Works in Therapy*. Washington, DC: American Psychological Association, 1999.

Hussain, Musharraf. *Five Pillars of Islam: Laying the Foundations of Divine Love and Service to Humanity*. Leicestershire, UK: Kube, 2012.

Jampolsky, Lee L. "Healing the Addictive Mind." In *Addiction and Spirituality: A Multidisciplinary Approach*, edited by Oliver J. Morgan and Merle Jordan, 55–74. Danvers, MA: Chalice, 1999.

Jung, Carl G. *The Development of Personality: Papers on Child Psychology, Education and Related Subjects*. The Collected Works of C. G. Jung 17. New York: Princeton University Press, 1954.

Kabat-Zinn, Jon. *Wherever You Go There You Are: Mindfulness Meditation in Everyday Life*. New York: Hyperion, 1994.

Kasser, Tim, et al. "Changes in Materialism, Changes in Psychological Well-Being: Evidence from Three Longitudinal Studies and an Intervention Experiment." *Motivation and Emotion* 38.1 (2013) 1–22. http://dx.doi.org/10.1007/s11031-013-9371-4.

Khan, Maulana Wahiduddin. "Simplicity Is a Part of Faith." *The Sunday Guardian*, December 7, 2013. https://www.sunday-guardian.com/analysis/simplicity-is-a-part-of-faith.

Kierkegaard, Søren. *The Sickness Unto Death*. Princeton: Princeton University Press, 1941.

Knapp, Caroline. *Drinking: A Love Story*. New York: Dial, 1996.

Kogan, Marcela. "Where Happiness Lies: Social Scientists Reveal Their Research Findings in the Realm of Positive Psychology." *American*

Bibliography

Psychological Association 32.1 (2001) 74. https://www.apa.org/monitor/jan01/positivepsych.

Kurtz, Ernest, and Katherine Ketcham. *The Spirituality of Imperfection.* New York: Bantam, 1992.

Lamott, Anne. *Bird by Bird: Some Instructions on Writing and Life.* New York: Random House, 1994.

Lerner, Harriet Goldhor. *The Dance of Intimacy: A Woman's Guide to Courageous Acts of Change in Key Relationships.* New York: Harper & Row, 1989.

Lewis, C. S. *A Grief Observed.* London: Faber & Faber, 1961.

———. *The Problem of Pain.* New York, Macmillan, 1962.

Loya, Joseph, et al. *The Tao of Jesus.* New Jersey: Paulist, 1998.

Malone, Thomas P., and Patrick Thomas Malone. *The Art of Intimacy.* New York: Prentis Hall, 1987.

Martin, James. *The Jesuit Guide to Almost Everything: A Spirituality for Real Life.* New York: Harper Collins, 2010.

May, Gerald. *Addiction and Grace.* San Francisco: Harper & Row, 1988.

McClone, Kevin P. "Intimacy and Healthy Affective Maturity: Guidelines for Formation." *Human Development* 30.4 (Winter 2009) 5–13.

———. "The Psychospirituality of Addiction." *Seminary Journal* 9 (Winter 2003) 21–29.

———. *Relationship of Core Spiritual Experiences and Sense of Coherence to Grief Experiences in Response to the Death of a Significant Other: A Clinical Research Project.* Illinois School of Professional Psychology, Chicago, IL, April 1997.

Meichenbaum, Donald. *Roadmap to Resilience: A Guide for Military, Trauma Victims and Their Families.* Vermont: Crown, 2012.

Merton, Thomas. *Love and Living.* Edited by Naomi Burton Stone and Brother Patrick Hart. New York: Harcourt Brace Jovanovich, 1979.

———. *My Argument with the Gestapo: A Maccaronic Journal.* New Directions: New York, 1969.

———. *New Seeds of Contemplation.* New York: New Directions, 1961.

———. *No Man Is an Island.* Boston: Shambhala, 1955.

———. *Seeds.* Selected and edited by Robert Inchausti. Boston: Shambala, 2002.

———. *Thoughts in Solitude.* New York: Harper Collins, 1956.

Morgan, Oliver J., and Merle Jordan, eds. *Addiction and Spirituality: A Multidisciplinary Approach.* Danvers, MA: Chalice, 1999.

Nouwen, Henri. *You Are the Beloved: Daily Meditations for Spiritual Living.* New York: Crown, 2017.

Oliver, Mary. *Swan: Poems and Prose Poems.* Boston: Beacon, 2010.

Palmer, Parker J. *On the Brink of Everything: Grace, Gravity & Getting Old.* California: Berrett-Koehler, 2018.

Peck, M. Scott. *The Road Less Travelled: A New Psychology of Love, Traditional Values and Spiritual Growth.* New York: Touchstone, 1978.

Polcino, Anna, ed. *Intimacy: Issues of Emotional Living in an Age of Stress for Clergy and Religious.* Worcester, MA: Affirmation, 1978.

Presnall, Lewis F. *The Search for Serenity and How to Achieve It.* Salt Lake City: Utah Alcoholism Foundation, 1959.

Rinpoche, Yongey Mingyur. *The Joy of Living: Unlocking the Secret & Science of Happiness.* New York: Three Rivers, 2007.

Rogers, Carl. *On Becoming a Person: A Therapist's View of Psychotherapy.* New York: Houghton Mifflin, 1961.

Rolheiser, Ronald. *The Holy Longing: The Search For a Christian Spirituality.* New York: Random House, 1999.

———. *Prayer: Our Deepest Longing.* Cincinnati: Franciscan Media, 2013.

———. *Sacred Fire: A Vision For a Deeper Human and Christian Maturity.* New York: Image, 2014.

Schultz, Duane P. *Growth Psychology: Models of the Healthy Personality.* New York: Van Nostrand Reinhold, 1977.

Seligman, Martin E. P., and Mihaly Csikszentmihalyi. "Positive Psychology: An Introduction." *American Psychologist* 55.1 (2000) 5–14. https://doi.org/10.1037/0003-066X.55.1.5.

Senge, Peter, et al. *Presence: Human Purpose and the Field of the Future.* New York: Crown, 2004.

Seppälä, Emma. "The Science Behind the Joy of Sharing Joy." *Psychology Today*, July 15, 2013. https://www.psychologytoday.com/us/blog/feeling-it/201307/the-science-behind-the-joy-sharing-joy.

Shi, David E. *The Simple Life: Plain Living and High Thinking in American Culture.* Oxford University Press: New York, 1985.

Solomon, Jenny. "Embracing Vulnerability: Parashat Shemot." *Dvar Torah* (blog), December 30, 2015. https://matankids.org/embracing-vulnerability-parashat-shemot/.

Storr, Antony. *Solitude: A Return to the Self.* New York: Ballantine, 1988.

"Study of Adult Development." https://www.adultdevelopmentstudy.org/grantandglueckstudy.

Teilhard de Chardin, Pierre. *The Phenomenon of Man.* London: Harper & Row, 1959.

Thoreau, Henry D. *Walden: An Annotated Edition.* Edited by Walter Harding. New York: Dover, 1995.

Tillich, Paul. *The Courage to Be.* New Haven: Yale University Press, 1952.

Tippett, Krista. "Lawrence Kushner: Kabbalah and Everyday Mysticism." *On Being*, May 15, 2014. https://onbeing.org/programs/lawrence-kushner-kabbalah-and-everyday-mysticism/.

Tournier, Paul. *The Meaning of Persons.* London: SCM, 1957.

"True Love." https://www.awakin.org/read/view.php?tid=216.

Twenge, Jean M. "The Age of Anxiety? Birth Cohort Change in Anxiety and Neuroticism, 1952–1993." *Case Western Reserve University; Journal of Personality and Social Psychology* 79.6 (2000) 1007–21.

Bibliography

Tzu, Lao. *Tao Teh Ching*. Translated by John C. Wu. New York: St. John's University Press, 1961.

Walsh, Bill. "The Science of Resilience." https://www.gse.harvard.edu/news/uk/15/03/science-resilience.

Whitehead, James, and Evelyn Eaton Whitehead. *Holy Eros: Pathways to a Passionate God*. New York: Orbis, 2009.

Wicks, Robert J. *Living a Gentle, Passionate Life*. New York: Paulist, 1998.

Wilson, Bill. *Language of the Heart: Bill Wilson's Grapevine Writings*. New York: Grapevine, 1988.

Winnicott, D. W. "The Capacity to Be Alone." *International Journal of Psychoanalysis* 39 (1958) 146–20. https://icpla.edu/wp-content/uploads/2012/10/Winnicott-D.-The-Capacity-to-be-Alone.pdf.

———. "Ego Distortion in Terms of True and False Self." In *The Maturational Processes and the Facilitating Environment: Studies in the Theory of Emotional Development*, 140–52. London, Routledge, 1984.

Made in the USA
Middletown, DE
08 August 2020